What people are saying

"Here at Citibank we use the Quick Course® computer training book series for 'just-in-time' job aids—the books are great for users who are too busy for tutorials and training. Quick Course® books provide very clear instruction and easy reference."

Bill Moreno, Development Manager
Citibank
San Francisco, CA

"At Geometric Results, much of our work is PC related and we need training tools that can quickly and effectively improve the PC skills of our people. Early this year we began using your materials in our internal PC training curriculum and the results have been outstanding. Both participants and instructors like the books and the measured learning outcomes have been very favorable."

Roger Hill, Instructional Systems Designer
Geometric Results Incorporated
Southfield, MI

"The concise and well organized text features numbered instructions, screen shots, and useful quick reference pointers, and tips…[This] affordable text is very helpful for educators who wish to build proficiency."

Computer Literacy column
Curriculum Administrator Magazine
Stamford, CT

"I have purchased five other books on this subject that I've probably paid more than $60 for, and your [Quick Course®] book taught me more than those five books combined!"

Emory Majors
Searcy, AR

"I would like you to know how much I enjoy the Quick Course® books I have received from you. The directions are clear and easy to follow with attention paid to every detail of the particular lesson."

Betty Weinkauf, Retired Senior
Mission, TX

QUICK COURSE®

in

MICROSOFT®

WORD 97

ONLINE PRESS INC.

Microsoft Press

PUBLISHED BY
Microsoft Press
A Division of Microsoft Corporation
One Microsoft Way
Redmond, WA 98052-6399

Library of Congress Cataloging-in-Publication Data

Quick Course in Microsoft Word 97 / Online Press Inc.
          p.   cm.
     Includes index.
     ISBN 1-57231-725-6
     1. Microsoft Word.   2. Word processing.   I. Online Press Inc.
     Z52.5.M52Q53   1997
     652.5'5369--dc21   97-27390
                                                                          CIP

Printed and bound in the United States of America.

1 2 3 4 5 6 7 8 9   WCWC   2 1 0 9 8 7

Distributed to the book trade in Canada by Macmillan of Canada, a division of Canada Publishing Corporation.

A CIP record of this book is available from the British Library.

Microsoft Press books are available through booksellers and distributors worldwide. For further information about international editions, contact your local Microsoft Corporation office. Or contact Microsoft Press International directly at fax (425) 936-7329. Visit our Web site at mspress.microsoft.com.

Quick Course® is a registered trademark of Online Press Inc. Windows and Microsoft are registered trademarks of Microsoft Corporation. Other product and company names mentioned herein may be the trademarks of their respective owners.

A Quick Course® Education/Training Edition for this title is published by Online Press Inc. For information about supplementary workbooks, contact Online Press Inc. at 14320 NE 21st St., Suite 18, Bellevue, WA, 98007, USA, 1-800-854-3344.

Authors: Joyce Cox and Christina Dudley of Online Press Inc., Bellevue, Washington
Acquisitions Editor: Susanne M. Freet
Project Editor: Maureen Williams Zimmerman

From the publisher

"I love these books!"

I can't tell you the number of times people have said those exact words to me about our new Quick Course® software training book series. And when I ask them what makes the books so special, this is what they say:

- **They're short and approachable, but they give you hours worth of good information.**

  Written for busy people with limited time, most Quick Course books are designed to be completed in 15 to 40 hours. Because Quick Course books are usually divided into two parts—Learning the Basics and Building Proficiency—users can selectively choose the chapters that meet their needs and complete them as time allows.

- **They're relevant and fun, and they assume you're no dummy.**

  Written in an easy-to-follow, step-by-step format, Quick Course books offer streamlined instruction for the new user in the form of no-nonsense, to-the-point tutorials and learning exercises. Each book provides a logical sequence of instructions for creating useful business documents—the same documents people use on the job. People can either follow along directly or substitute their own information and customize the documents. After finishing a book, users have a valuable "library" of documents they can continually recycle and update with new information.

- **They're direct and to the point, and they're a lot more than just pretty pictures.**

  Training-oriented rather than feature-oriented, Quick Course books don't cover the things you don't really need to know to do useful work. They offer easy-to-follow, step-by-step instructions; lots of screen shots for checking work in progress; quick-reference pointers for fast, easy lookup and review; and useful tips offering additional information on topics being discussed.

- **They're a rolled-into-one-book solution, and they meet a variety of training needs.**

  Designed with instructional flexibility in mind, Quick Course books can be used both for self-training and as the basis for weeklong courses, two-day seminars, and all-day workshops. They can be adapted to meet a variety of training needs, including classroom instruction, take-away practice exercises, and self-paced learning.

Microsoft Press is very excited about bringing you this extraordinary series. But you must be the judge. I hope you'll give these books a try. And maybe the next time I see you, you too will say, "Hey, Jim! I love these books!"

Jim Brown, Publisher
Microsoft Press

Content overview

PART ONE: LEARNING THE BASICS

PART TWO: BUILDING PROFICIENCY

Content details

PART ONE: LEARNING THE BASICS

ONE

LEARNING THE BASICS

In Part One, we cover basic techniques for working with Microsoft Word. After you have completed these three chapters, you will know enough to be able to handle the majority of documents you will create with Word. In Chapter 1, you learn how to work with the program while creating a business letter. In Chapter 2, you focus on editing techniques, including spell checking. Finally, in Chapter 3, you use some of Word's built-in templates and wizards to quickly create professional-looking documents, and then you experiment with some of Word's more advanced formatting capabilities.

1

Getting Started

While writing a simple business letter, we cover techniques for creating and saving documents, giving instructions using the mouse and the keyboard, applying formatting, printing, and getting help. Then we show you how to quit Word.

June 6, 1997

Fern Leaf, President
ChillFill Inc.
3500 NW Bay Street
Juneau, AK 99801

RE: GLACIER SERIES SLEEPING BAG LAUNCH PARTY

Dear Fern:

I am pleased to announce that In The Bag's **Glacier Series**, our latest line of sleeping bags, is now complete and ready for production. Thanks to the hard work of our development team, the product was finished ahead of schedule. I want to thank your company for its contribution to the product. The use of ChillFill insulation is instrumental in making Glacier bags so unique and exciting. Many retail stores have already placed large orders for these innovative, subzero-temperature sleeping bags.

We're throwing a party on Saturday, June 21, 1997 to honor those who contributed to the development of this excellent line. I will contact you next week with further details. I hope you will be able to attend.

Again, thank you!

Al Pine

I n this chapter, we show you how to save and retrieve documents, how to enter text and move around a document with reasonable efficiency, and how to select text so that you can do something with it. We cover all these topics while creating a short letter, and by the time you finish this chapter, you will know enough to create simple documents using Word. If you have used an earlier version of Word for Windows or you are familiar with other word-processing programs that run under Windows, you might be able to get by with quickly scanning this chapter for new features or Word-specific techniques.

We assume that you have installed Word on your computer and that you allowed the Setup program to stash everything where it belongs on your C: drive. We also assume that you have worked with Windows 95 before. If you are new to Windows 95, we recommend you take a look at *Quick Course® in Windows 95*, another book in our series, which will help you come up to speed in no time at all.

Creating a New Document

Well, let's jump right in and create our first Word document:

1. With Windows 95 loaded, click the Start button.

2. Choose Microsoft Word from the Programs submenu.

When the program opens, you see a window like the one shown at the top of the facing page. (Your screen may look slightly different from ours depending on your computer's settings—for example, the ruler, Office Assistant, and non-printing characters may be turned on or off. We'll discuss these elements as the book progresses. Also, Microsoft Office users may see the Office shortcut bar at the top of their screen. See the adjacent tip for information about how to use buttons on this bar to start Word.)

Other ways to start Word

Instead of starting Word by choosing it from the Start menu, you can create a shortcut icon for Word on your desktop. Right-click an open area of the desktop and choose New and then Shortcut from the object menu. In the Create Shortcut dialog box, click the Browse button, navigate to Program Files/Micfosoft Office/Microsoft Word, and click Next. Then type a name for the shortcut icon and click Finish. (To delete a shortcut icon, simply drag it to the Recycle Bin.) For maximum efficiency, you can start Word and open a recently used document by choosing Documents from the Start menu and then choosing the document from the Documents submenu, where Windows 95 stores the names of up to 15 of the most recently opened files. If you are using Microsoft Office and have installed the Microsoft Office shortcut bar, you can click the Open Office Document button on the Office shortcut bar and navigate to the folder in which the document you want to open is stored, or you can choose Open Office Document from the top of the Start menu. To start Word and open a new document, you can click the New Office Document button on the Office shortcut bar and then double-click the Blank Document icon, or you can choose New Office Document from the top of the Start menu.

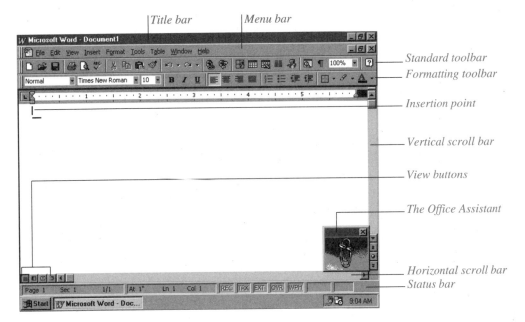

Title bar *Menu bar*

Standard toolbar
Formatting toolbar
Insertion point
Vertical scroll bar
View buttons
The Office Assistant
Horizontal scroll bar
Status bar

You'll learn what all the labeled parts of the window are as we work our way through this chapter.

Entering Text

Let's start by writing a paragraph. Follow these steps:

1. If the Office Assistant displays a list of options for you, click the Start Microsoft Word option to start Word. If the Assistant appears by itself, click its Close button (the one with the X) to remove it from the screen. (We'll discuss the Office Assistant in more detail on page 26.) The blinking *insertion point* indicates where the next character you type will appear on the screen. Type the following:

I am pleased to announce that In The Bag's Glacier Series, our latest line of sleeping bags, is now complete and ready for production. Thanks to the hard work of our development team, the product was finished ahead of schedule. I want to thank your company for its contribution to the product. The use of ChillFill insulation is instrumental in making Glacier bags so unique and exciting. Many retail stores have already placed large orders for these innovative, subzero-temperature sleeping bags.

Correcting mistakes

Word corrects some simple typos, such as *teh* (the) and *adn* (and); we explain how on page 37. If you spell a less common word incorrectly—or if you use proper nouns or other correct but obscure spellings—Word points out the mistake with a red, wavy underline. If Word thinks you've made a grammatical mistake, it uses a green, wavy underline. We show you some editing techniques on page 20, but in the meantime, if you make a mistake and want to correct it, simply press the Backspace key until you've deleted the error and then retype the text.

Word wrapping

As each line of text reaches the right edge of the screen, the next word you type moves to a new line. This is called *word wrapping*. When entering text in Word, you don't have to worry about pressing the Enter key to end one line and start another. Word takes care of that chore for you, filling each line with as many words as will fit. (As you follow our examples, don't worry if your word wrapping isn't identical to ours.)

2. Press Enter to end the paragraph. Your screen looks like this:

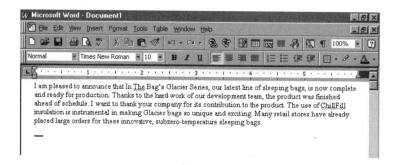

Now that we have a little text on the screen, we have something to work with. First let's cover some navigation basics.

Moving Around

We need to know how to move around a document for two reasons: so that we can view a document that is too long to fit on the screen, and so that we can edit its text.

Scrolling

The document window is often not big enough to display all of its contents. To bring out-of-sight information into view, we use the scroll bars. Clicking the arrow at the end of a scroll bar moves the window's contents a small distance in the direction of the arrow. Clicking on either side of a scroll box (both of which are now at the ends of their scroll bars) moves the contents one windowful. The position of the scroll box in relation to the scroll bar indicates the position of the window in relation to its contents. Drag the scroll box to see specific parts of a document—for example, the middle or end. (As we move the vertical scroll box in a multi-page document, Word displays the corresponding page number in a box beside the scroll bar.)

When it comes to editing, the insertion point is where the action is. Clicking anywhere in the text on the screen moves the insertion point to that location, or we can move the insertion point with the navigation keys, like this:

Navigation keys

To move the insertion point...	Press...
One character left or right	Left Arrow or Right Arrow
One word left or right	Ctrl+Left Arrow or Ctrl+Right Arrow
One line up or down	Up or Down Arrow
One paragraph up or down	Ctrl+Up Arrow or Ctrl+Down Arrow
One screenful up or down	PageUp or PageDown
To left or right end of current line	Home or End
To first or last character in document	Ctrl+Home or Ctrl+End
To previous editing location	Shift+F5

(In this book, we indicate that two or more keys are to be pressed together by separating the key names with a plus sign. For example, *press Ctrl+Home* means hold down the Ctrl key while simultaneously pressing the Home key.)

Selecting Text

Before we can do much with this paragraph, we need to discuss how to select text. Knowing how to select text efficiently saves time because we can then edit or format all the selected text at once, instead of a letter or word at a time. The simplest way to learn how to select text is to actually do it, so follow these steps to select some text blocks:

1. Move the pointer to the word *finished* and double-click it. The word changes to white on black (called *highlighting*) to indicate that it is selected, as shown on the next page.

Whole word selection

By default, Word selects whole words. For example, if you start a selection in the middle of a word and drag beyond the last character, Word selects the entire word. If you drag to the first character of the next word, Word selects that word, and so on. You can tell Word to select only the characters you drag across by choosing Options from the Tools menu, clicking the Edit tab, clicking the When Selecting Automatically Select Entire Word option to deselect it, and clicking OK.

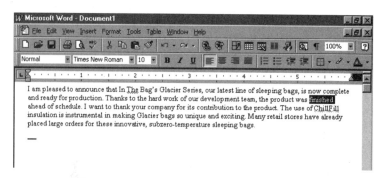

2. Point to the left of *ChillFill* and click the left mouse button to position the insertion point at the beginning of the word. Then point to the right of *insulation*, hold down the Shift key, and click the left mouse button. (This action is sometimes referred to as *Shift-clicking*.) Word highlights the words between the two clicks:

Shift-clicking

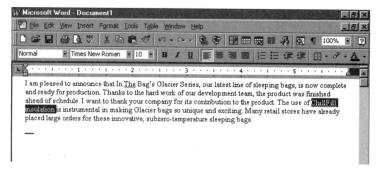

Selecting by dragging

3. Point to the left of the word *innovative*, hold down the left mouse button, drag to the right until *innovative, subzero-temperature sleeping bags* is selected, and release the mouse button. Using this technique, you can highlight exactly as much or as little text as you need.

4. Click an insertion point to the left of the *T* in *Thanks*. Hold down the Shift key, press the Right Arrow key until the entire word is highlighted, and release the Shift key.

5. Without moving the selection, hold down the Shift key again, press the Down Arrow key, and then press the Left or Right Arrow key until the entire sentence is highlighted, like this:

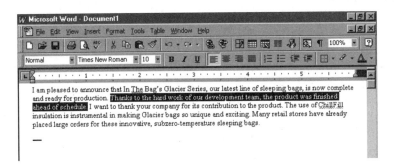

6. Next, try pressing different Arrow keys while holding down the Shift key. As long as you hold down Shift, Word extends the selection in the direction of the key's arrow.

7. Release the Shift key and press Home to move the insertion point to the beginning of the line where the selection starts. Moving the insertion point removes any highlighting.

8. Move the mouse pointer to the far left side of the window. When the pointer changes to an arrow, it is in an invisible vertical strip called the *selection bar*.

The selection bar

9. Position the arrow pointer in the selection bar adjacent to the line that contains the word *ChillFill* and click the left mouse button once. Word highlights the line as shown here:

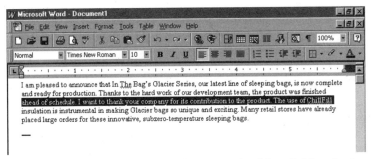

10. Now highlight the entire paragraph by double-clicking in the selection bar next to the paragraph.

We can also drag the pointer in the selection bar to select multiple lines or paragraphs. To select all of the paragraphs in a document, we can triple-click in the selection bar.

Using an IntelliMouse

If you have the Microsoft Intelli-Mouse, you can scroll up or down in a document by rotating the wheel between the left and right mouse buttons forward or backward. For continuous scrolling, hold down the wheel button and drag the pointer above or below the origin mark (the dot with the arrows). You can control your scrolling speed by moving the pointer toward or away from the origin mark. To zoom in or out on a page, hold down the Ctrl key as you move the wheel forward or backward.

Giving Instructions

Now that we know how to select text, let's discuss how we tell Word what to do with the selection. We give instructions by clicking buttons on toolbars, by choosing menu commands, and by pressing keyboard shortcuts.

Using the Toolbars

Word comes with a set of toolbars, each with a set of tools that are appropriate for a particular type of task. At the moment, we can see the Standard and Formatting toolbars. More specialized buttons are gathered together on other toolbars, which we can display at any time (see page 14). We can also hide the toolbars if we need to view more of a document at once. Let's explore the toolbars:

ToolTips

1. Point to each button in turn, pausing until the name appears in a box below the pointer. This helpful feature is called *ToolTips*.

2. Use any of the methods discussed on pages 7 and 8 to select the first occurrence of *Glacier Series*.

The Bold, Underline, and Italic buttons

3. Click the Bold button on the Formatting toolbar and then click the Underline button. (You could also add italic formatting by clicking the Italic button.)

4. Press Home to remove the highlighting. As you can see, these two simple changes really make the text stand out:

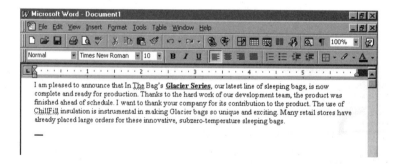

Now let's experiment with the document's font and font size:

Changing the font

1. Select the paragraph and click the arrow to the right of the Font box to display a list of the available fonts.

2. If necessary, use the scroll bar on the right side of the drop-down list to bring the top of the list into view and then click Arial. The font of the text changes, and the setting in the Font box now reflects the new font.

3. With the paragraph still selected, click the arrow to the right of the Font Size box and then click 12 in the drop-down list.

Changing the font size

4. Now press End so that you can see the results:

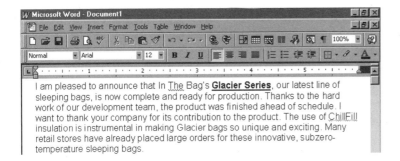

We have just used toolbar buttons and boxes to apply common character formats to a text selection. *Character formats* affect the appearance of individual characters. They can be applied to any number of characters, from one to the whole document. We can also use toolbar buttons to change *paragraph formats*, which, as their name suggests, affect the appearance of an entire paragraph. Let's see how changing the alignment of a paragraph affects the way it looks:

1. Press Ctrl+Home to move to the beginning of the document, and then type the following, pressing Enter to end paragraphs and create blank lines where indicated, and pressing Enter twice after the salutation:

June 6, 1997 (Press Enter)

Fern Leaf, President (Press Enter)

ChillFill Inc. (Press Enter)

3500 NW Bay Street (Press Enter)

Juneau, AK 99801 (Press Enter)

(Press Enter)

RE: GLACIER SERIES SLEEPING BAG LAUNCH PARTY

(Press Enter twice)

Dear Fern: (Press Enter twice)

More about toolbars

You may have noticed that some toolbars appear "docked" at the top, bottom, or sides of the window while others "float" somewhere over the window. To convert a docked toolbar to a floating toolbar, double-click the left end of a horizontal toolbar or the top of a vertical toolbar. Double-clicking the title bar of a floating toolbar docks it to an edge of the window. You can also move the floating toolbar to a new position on the screen by dragging its title bar. If you drag it to the top, sides, or bottom of the screen, the toolbar arranges itself along that edge of the document window. To return a toolbar to its original location, simply drag it back to that spot. You can also customize toolbars; see the tip on page 15.

The Align Right button

The Center button

2. If the Office Assistant appears, click the second option to continue writing the letter without help.

3. Press Crtl+Home and click the Align Right button to right-align the date.

4. Click an insertion point anywhere in the subject (RE:) line and then click the Center button. Here are the results:

Using Menu Commands

Most of the buttons on the toolbars have equivalent commands on Word's menus, which are arranged on the menu bar that spans the window below the title bar. In addition, we can choose some commands from object menus, which appear when we click elements of the document or the window using the right mouse button. We look at both types of menus in this section.

Buttons vs. commands

So when do we use a button and when do we use a command? We can always use a command to carry out a particular task, but we can't always use a corresponding button. Clicking the button often carries out its associated command with its predefined, or default, settings without any further input from us. When a command is not represented by a toolbar button, or when we want to use a command with something other than its default settings, we need to choose the command from a menu.

Choosing Menu Bar Commands

Because the procedure for choosing menu commands is the same for all Windows applications, we assume that you are

Menu command buttons

You might have noticed that for some menu commands, an icon appears to the left of the command name. The icon simply indicates that a corresponding button exists for this command on one of Word's toolbars.

familiar with it. If you are a new Windows user, we suggest that you spend a little time becoming familiar with the mechanics of menus, commands, and dialog boxes before proceeding. Here, we'll run through the steps for choosing a command and do some useful exploring at the same time:

1. Click View on the menu bar to display this menu:

The View menu provides commands for customizing the screen display. The first five commands control which "view" the document is displayed in. Notice that the button icon next to the Normal command appears pressed, indicating that, of these five commands, Normal is the command currently in effect—in other words, the document is displayed in normal view. Choosing another of these five commands puts that command into effect and deactivates Normal.

◄———— Mutually exclusive commands

2. Choose the Ruler command from the View menu by clicking the name to turn off the ruler. Word hides the ruler below the Formatting toolbar. (If your ruler was already turned off, choosing Ruler turns it on. Choose the command a second time to turn it back off.)

◄———— Turning the ruler on/off

3. Click the View menu again and notice that the Ruler command no longer has a check mark next to its name, indicating that the command is turned off. Commands that can be turned on and off are called *toggle commands*. Choosing a checked toggle command turns off the command without affecting the status of any other command.

4. Choose the Ruler command to turn on the ruler.

Reappearing ruler

When the ruler is turned off, you can temporarily view it by pointing to the gray bar below the toolbars. The ruler drops down and remains visible as long as the pointer is over it. When you move the pointer away from it, the ruler disappears.

Turning toolbars on/off

5. Click the View menu again (notice that a check mark has reappeared next to Ruler) and point to the Toolbars command, which has a right-pointing arrowhead next to its name. Pointing to the command displays this *submenu* of additional commands, which you can choose simply by clicking them in the usual way:

Submenus

6. Click AutoText to display the AutoText toolbar.

7. Click the View menu again and choose Toolbars and then Customize to display this *dialog box*:

Dialog boxes

When you choose a command that is followed by an ellipsis on the menu, you have to supply additional information by setting options in a dialog box before Word can carry out the command.

Notice that the Customize dialog box is multilayered, with each layer designated at the top of the dialog box by a tab like a file folder tab. The Toolbars tab is currently displayed. (If it's not, click Toolbars at the top of the dialog box.)

8. Turn off the AutoText toolbar by clicking its checked box. Then click the four check boxes below the Formatting check box to turn them on, and click Close. (If you need to move a toolbar away from the Customize dialog box, point to its title bar, hold down the left mouse button, and drag it to the desired location.) Your screen should look something like the one below. Notice that toolbars can appear across the top or bottom of the window, down the sides, or floating over the workspace. (See the tip on page 11 for more information about toolbars.)

Moving toolbars

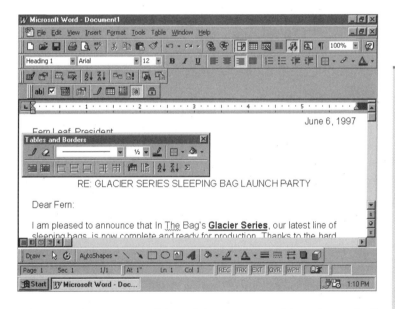

9. Use ToolTips to get an idea of the names and functions of all the buttons on the new toolbars.

Choosing Object Menu Commands

For efficiency, the commands we are likely to use with a particular object, such as a block of text, are combined on

The other Customize options

Four buttons on the right side of the Toolbars tab in the Customize dialog box give you more customization options. Click New to create your own toolbar and then click the Commands tab and add buttons to your toolbar by dragging command names to it. (Delete buttons by dragging them away.) Back on the Toolbars tab, you can click the Rename or Delete buttons to rename or delete your custom toolbar. (You cannot rename or delete toolbars that come with Word.) If you have customized a Word toolbar and want to return it to its default settings, simply select the toolbar in the Toolbars list and click the Reset button. You can also set custom keyboard shortcuts by clicking the Keyboard button at the bottom of the Customize dialog box.

Object menus →

Right-clicking →

special menus, called *object menus*. Object menus are also available for window elements, such as the toolbars. We access an object menu by pointing to the object and clicking the right mouse button. This action is called *right-clicking*. Try the following:

1. Point to one of the toolbars, right-click to display the toolbar object menu, and choose Database from the menu to turn off the Database toolbar.

2. Right-click a toolbar to display the object menu again. You don't want to repeat step 1 to turn off the toolbars one at a time, so choose Customize from the bottom of the menu to display the dialog box you saw earlier, deselect all the check boxes except Standard and Formatting, and click Close.

Using Keyboard Shortcuts

We can't imagine anyone wanting to work with Word using only the keyboard. Using a mouse makes working with most Windows applications much easier, and Word is no exception. However, if our hands are already on the keyboard, using keyboard shortcuts to access commands can be more efficient. We have already used the Ctrl+Home keyboard shortcut to move to the top of the document now on the screen. Here are a few more examples:

Help with shortcuts

The list of keyboard shortcuts is extensive, and it would take a lot of space to reproduce it here. For more information about keyboard shortcuts, ask the Office Assistant or choose Contents And Index from the Help menu, and on the Index tab, type *keys* in the Type The First Few Letters box. Then click Shortcut Keys in the Check The Index Entry box and click Display. In the Topics Found window, click the entry for the type of task you are interested in and click Display again. (See page 26 for more information about online help.)

1. Select the subject line (*RE: GLACIER SERIES SLEEPING BAG LAUNCH PARTY*) and press first Ctrl+B and then Ctrl+U to make the line bold and underlined. (As you know, you can achieve the same effect by clicking the Bold and Underline buttons on the Formatting toolbar.)

2. Now use a keyboard shortcut to change the alignment of the first paragraph you typed. Click an insertion point in the paragraph that begins *I am pleased* and press Ctrl+J to justify it so that its lines are even with both the left and right margins. (Pressing Ctrl+L would left-align the paragraph, Ctrl+R would right-align it, and Ctrl+E would center it.)

3. Press Ctrl+Home to move the insertion point to the top of the document. The results are shown on the facing page:

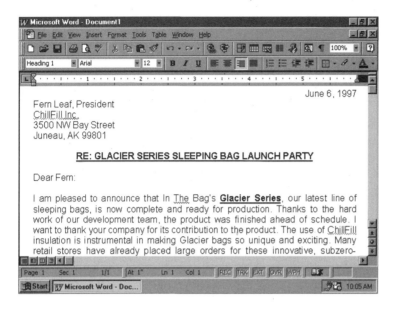

Saving Documents

Until we save the document we have created as a file on a disk, the document exists only in the computer's memory and disappears if the computer is intentionally or unintentionally turned off. To save the document for the first time, we can click the Save button or choose Save As from the File menu to display a dialog box in which we specify a name for the document. Let's save the document now on the screen:

1. Choose Save As from the File menu to display the Save As dialog box:

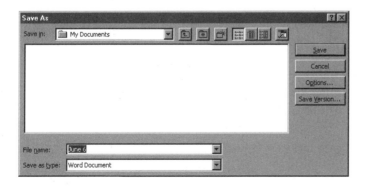

2. Word suggests *June 6*, the first "phrase" in the document, as the filename. With *June 6* highlighted, type *ChillFill Letter*

Saving options

The document will be saved in the folder designated in the Save In box. If you want to store the document in a different folder, click the arrow to the right of the Save In box, use the drop-down list to navigate to the folder in which you want the document to be saved, and double-click that folder to display its name in the Save In box before you click Save to save the document. To save a document in a format other than that of a normal Word document, select the format you want from the Save As Type drop-down list. For example, to save a document in ASCII (text-only) format so that it can be opened in other applications, choose Save As from the File menu, name the document, select Text Only from the Save As Type list, and click Save. (ASCII means American Standard Code for Information Interchange.)

Filename specifications ———————▶

in the File Name edit box. (Word 97 can handle long file-names, meaning that the filenames can have up to 255 characters, and they can contain spaces. They cannot contain the < > : * | \ " " ? and / characters.)

3. Click Save to save the document in the My Documents folder on your hard drive.

The Save button ———————————▶

From now on, we can click the Save button any time we want to save changes to this document. Because Word knows the name of the document, it simply saves the file by overwriting the old version with the new version.

More Ways to Create New Documents

Part of the magic of a computer is that we can use the same information for different purposes without retyping the information each time. When we have already created one document and we want to adapt it for a different purpose without destroying the original, we can create a copy by saving the document with a new name. The original document remains unaltered under its own filename. Try this:

1. Choose Save As from the File menu.

2. Replace the name in the File Name edit box by typing *Launch Party Letter*, and click Save. Word creates a copy of the file, closes the original ChillFill Letter, and changes the filename in the title bar to Launch Party Letter.

We can create a totally new document at any time without closing any open documents. Follow these steps:

The New button ———————————▶

1. Click the New button on the Standard toolbar. Word displays a new document called Document2, completely obscuring Launch Party Letter, which is still open.

2. Type the following paragraph, misspelling *Saturday* and *honor* (Word will underline them with red, wavy lines):

We're throwing a party on **Saterday**, *June 21, 1997 to* **honur** *those who contributed to the development of this excellent line. I hope that you will be able to attend. I will contact you with more details next week.*

3. Press Enter and then save the document with the name *Glacier Bag Party*.

Opening Documents

We now have a couple of open documents in separate, stacked windows. For good measure, let's open an existing document by following these steps:

1. Click the Open button on the Standard toolbar to display the dialog box shown here:

The Open button

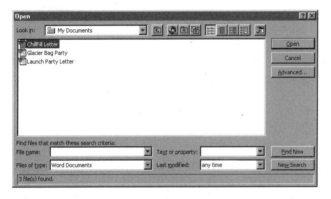

2. With ChillFill Letter selected, click Open.

Manipulating Windows

We'll pause here to review some window basics. Follow these steps to move from one window to another:

1. Choose Launch Party Letter from the list of open documents at the bottom of the Window menu. That document comes to the top of the stack of windows.

2. Choose Arrange All from the Window menu. The three open documents arrange themselves so that they each occupy a third of the screen as shown on the next page.

Finding documents

At the bottom of the Open dialog box are boxes that provide easy ways of locating the document you need. Suppose you can't remember exactly what you called the ChillFill Letter document or where you stored it. Simply navigate to the folder for your C: drive, click the New Search button, enter *ChillFill* in the File Name edit box, and click the Commands And Settings button at the top of the dialog box. Then choose Search Subfolders from the drop-down menu to tell Word to look in all the folders on your C: drive. Word searches this drive and its subfolders for any Word documents with *ChillFill* in the filename and lists the ones it finds. You can then select the document you want and click the Open button. If you have many documents with similar names, you can refine the search by specifying text included in the document or its date of modification, or you can click the Advanced button and specify additional criteria. You can also save searches in the Advanced Find dialog box.

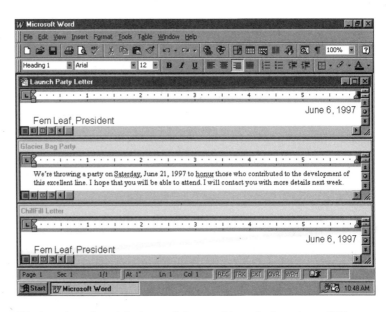

Notice that the title bar of the active window is a different color than those of the inactive windows. Any entries you make and most commands you choose will affect only the document in the active window.

3. Click anywhere in Glacier Bag Party to activate it, and then click the Glacier Bag Party window's Maximize button (the middle of the three buttons at the right end of the window's title bar). The window expands to fill the screen, completely obscuring Launch Party Letter and ChillFill Letter.

Simple Editing

When creating documents, we will usually start by typing roughly what we want the document to contain and then we'll go back and edit the contents until we are satisfied with them. In this section, we'll quickly cover some basic editing techniques.

Deleting and Replacing Text

First let's make a few small changes. Follow these steps:

1. Click an insertion point to the left of the *e* in *Saterday*, press the Delete (Del) key to delete the character to the right, and without moving the insertion point, type *u*. The red, wavy underline that flags the typo disappears.

Document management

With Word 97, you can manage your documents from within the Word program. You can delete, rename, or move your documents from Word's Open or Save As dialog box. For example, by right-clicking a filename in the Open dialog box, you can choose from several object-menu commands that allow you to print the document, send a copy of the document to a floppy disk, delete the document, or rename it. You can perform most of these tasks from the Save As dialog box as well. In addition, if you want to save your document in a folder that doesn't yet exist, you can click the Create New Folder button at the top of the Save As dialog box and create the folder as part of the save operation.

2. Click an insertion point to the right of the *u* in *honur*, press the Backspace key to delete the character to the left, and then type *o*.

3. Select the word *that* in the second line, and press either Delete or Backspace to delete the word.

4. Double-click the word *more* in the second line and, with the word highlighted, type *further* as its replacement.

5. Click the Save button to save Glacier Bag Party.

Moving and Copying Text

We can move or copy any amount of text within the same document or to a different document. Move operations can be carried out using the Cut and Paste buttons on the Standard toolbar. Similarly, copy operations can be carried out using the Copy and Paste buttons. Let's experiment:

1. In Glacier Bag Party, select the words *next week* and click the Cut button. Word removes the text from the document and stores it in a temporary storage place, called the *Clipboard*, in your computer's memory.

The Cut button

2. Click an insertion point to the left of the *w* in *with* and click the Paste button. Word inserts the cut text, preceding it with a space.

The Paste button

3. Then select the sentence that begins *I hope you* and click the Cut button.

4. Click an insertion point to the right of the very last period in the text and click the Paste button.

Now let's try copying text to a different document:

1. Choose Select All from the Edit menu to select all the text in Glacier Bag Party, and then click the Copy button.

The Copy button

2. Choose Launch Party Letter from the Window menu to activate the letter.

3. Press Ctrl+End to move to the end of the letter, press Enter to add a blank line, and then click the Paste button to insert the selected paragraph.

When we copied the paragraph from Glacier Bag Party to Launch Party Letter, we copied the formatting of the paragraph as well. We'll reformat the entire letter in a moment.

Undoing and Redoing Commands

For those occasions when we make an editing mistake, Word provides a safety net: the Undo command. Try this:

The Undo button

The Redo button

1. You're not sure you need the paragraph you copied into the letter, so click the Undo button to reverse the paste operation from the previous steps.

2. Change your mind again, and click the Redo button to paste the paragraph back into the letter.

Printing Documents

Whether we are writing a letter, a newsletter, or an annual report, the end product of many of our Word sessions will be a printout. If you can print from any other Windows application, you should have no trouble printing from Word. First, let's finish off the letter:

1. With the insertion point at the end of the letter, type *Again, thank you!*, press Enter four times, type *Al Pine*, and press Enter again.

Undoing and redoing multiple actions

In Word, you can undo and redo several actions at a time. Click the arrow to the right of the appropriate button and drag through the actions in the list that you want to undo or redo. You cannot undo or redo a single action other than the last one. For example, to undo the third action in the list, you must also undo the first and second.

2. Choose Select All from the Edit menu, and change the Font setting on the Formatting toolbar to Times New Roman and the Font Size setting to 10.

3. Finally, select the second paragraph and click the Justify button on the Formatting toolbar.

4. Press Ctrl+Home and then save the letter, which now looks like the one shown here:

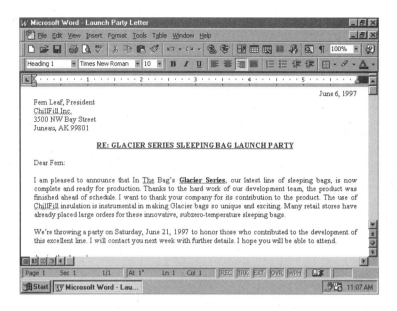

Previewing Documents

The letter we have written is only one page long and it has no headers or footers. However, it is worth checking even a document this small in print preview to get an idea of how it looks on the page. Follow these steps to preview the letter:

1. Click the Print Preview button on the Standard toolbar to display the entire page as shown here:

The Print Preview button

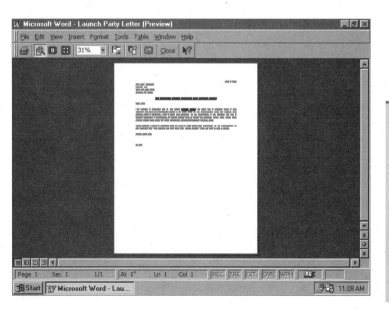

Editing in print preview

Suppose you zoom in on a section of a document and notice something you need to change. To edit a document while in print preview, click the Magnifier button on the Print Preview toolbar to change the pointer to an insertion point. Make your changes and click the Magnifier button again. Then click the document to zoom out.

Zooming in and out

2. Move the mouse pointer over the letter and when the pointer changes to a magnifying glass, click the left mouse button to zoom in on the letter. Click the mouse button again to zoom out.

3. Click the Close button on the Print Preview toolbar.

Changing Page Layout

Adjusting margins

Let's modify the page layout by widening the top and side margins so that the letter sits lower and takes up more of the page. Follow these steps:

1. Choose Page Setup from the File menu to display the dialog box shown here:

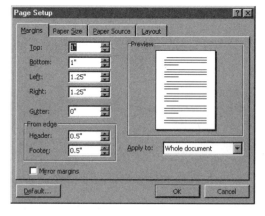

> **More print specifications**
>
> If you don't want Word to collate the copies when printing multiple copies, click the Collate check box to deselect it. To print only the page containing the insertion point, click the Current Page option. To print selected pages, click the Pages option and then enter the page numbers (for example, *2-4* for pages 2, 3, and 4; and *2,4* for pages 2 and 4 only). In the Print What drop-down list, specify what you want to print. In the Print drop-down list, specify whether you want to print all, all odd, or all even pages. Click the Print To File check box to "print" an image of the document to a file on disk. Clicking Properties displays a tabbed dialog box with still more printing options, including the ability to print several small pages on one piece of paper in such a way that the paper can be folded to produce booklets of two or four pages. You can also change the page orientation from Portrait (vertical) to Landscape (horizontal) here, or you can use the Orientation setting on the Paper Size tab of the Page Setup dialog box.

2. With the Top setting highlighted, type *1.5*, and press the Tab key twice to skip over the Bottom setting and highlight the Left setting.

3. Type *1.5* as the new Left setting, press Tab, type *1.5* as the new Right setting, and press Tab again.

4. Notice the effects of your changes in the sample to the right and then click OK to return to the letter.

5. Click the Print Preview button to see how the letter looks, and then click Close to return to normal view.

Straightforward Printing

We can print directly from print preview by clicking the Print button on the Print Preview toolbar, but here's how to print a document from normal view:

1. Click the Print button on the Standard toolbar.

The Print button

Word prints the active document with the default settings: one copy of the entire document. To print multiple copies or to print selected pages, we must use the Print command on the File menu instead of the Print button on the toolbar. Follow these steps:

1. Choose Print from the File menu to display this dialog box:

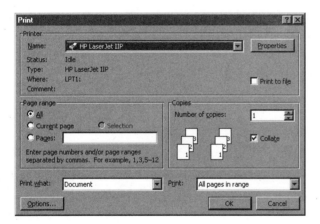

Notice that the Print dialog box tells you which printer Word will use.

2. In the Copies section, type *2* to replace the default setting of 1 in the Number Of Copies edit box.

3. Click the Pages option in the Page Range section and type *1-3* in the edit box to tell Word to print pages 1 through 3 only.

4. We aren't actually going to print using these specifications, so click Cancel to close the Print dialog box.

Rather than explain the other printing options in detail here (see the adjacent tip), we'll move on to the next section, where

Setting up for printing

When you installed Windows, the Setup program also installed the driver (the control program) for the printer attached to your computer. If you also have access to other printers, you can install their drivers by using the Add Printer Wizard in the Printers folder. (Choose Settings and then Printers from the Start menu.) The installed printers can all be accessed by Word, but only one at a time. To switch printers, choose Print from the File menu, click the arrow to the right of the Name box in the Printer section of the Print dialog box, select the printer you want to use, and click OK.

we show you how to get information about these options and other Word features.

Getting Help

Are you worried that you might not remember everything we've covered so far? Don't be. If we forget how to carry out a particular task, help is never far away. You've already seen how the ToolTips feature and the descriptions in the status bar can jog your memory about the functions of the toolbar buttons. And you may have noticed that the dialog boxes contain a Help button—the ? in the top right corner—you can click to get information about their options. Here we'll look at ways to get information using the Office Assistant, a new feature of Word 97, which you've probably seen pop-up a few times already. Follow these steps:

Help with dialog boxes

The Office Assistant button

1. Click the Office Assistant button on the Standard toolbar. The Office Assistant appears, giving you several options for proceeding, as shown here:

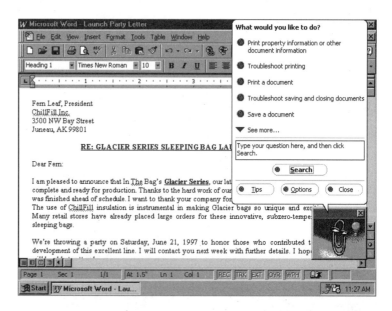

Because printing was the last procedure you completed, the Office Assistant's options are currently based on the topic of printing. (If you don't find any of the current options helpful, you can type a question in the Search box and then click the

Search button to have the Office Assistant find topics that most closely match your question.)

2. Click the Print A Document option to display the Help window shown below. (It may take a few seconds while the help file is being prepared.)

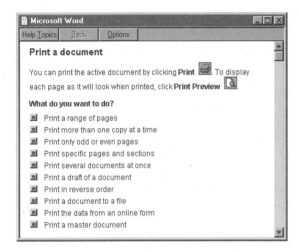

More about the Office Assistant

The Office Assistant button displays a light bulb when the Office Assistant has a tip for you. Click the button and then click the light bulb in the Office Assistant box to see the tip. If you want to leave the Office Assistant open, you can move it by dragging its title bar, and you can size it by dragging its frame (only two sizes are available). You can display the search box at any time by clicking the title bar. If having the Office Assistant on the screen bothers you, or if you would like to customize it, you can click the Office Assistant's Options button to open the Office Assistant dialog box. Here, you can select and deselect various options that control when the Office Assistant appears, whether it makes sounds, and what tips it displays. If you want the Office Assistant to appear only when you click the Office Assistant button on the Standard toolbar, deselect the Respond To F1 Key, Help With Wizards, and Display Alerts options in the Assistant Capabilities section on the Options tab. On the Gallery tab, you can click the Next button to scroll through the different animated choices for the assistant (the default is the paper clip) and then click OK to change the assistant. (You may need to insert your Office CD-ROM to complete the switch.)

3. Read through the information and then click the arrow to the left of the Print A Range Of Pages option to display these instructions on how to complete the task:

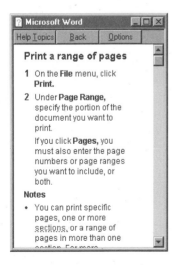

4. Click the Back button to return to the Print A Document topic, and explore other options.

5. Click the Help window's Close button (the one with the X) and then close the Office Assistant using the same method.

If you prefer to get information without the aid of the Office Assistant, you can simply use the Help menu. Follow the steps below:

Searching the Help contents

1. Choose Contents And Index from the Help menu. On the Contents tab, you can look up information by category. (Double-click book icons to display subcategories, and then select a topic and click Display.)

Searching the Help index

2. Click the Index tab to display this dialog box:

3. In the edit box, type *printi*. The list below scrolls to display topics beginning with the letters you type.

4. In the list of printing topics, select Documents and click the Display button. Then in the Topics Found window, select Print A Document and click Display again. Help offers the information shown on page 27.

5. Close the Help window.

We'll leave you to explore other Help topics on your own.

Using the Web for help

If you have a modem and are connected to the Internet, you can access Microsoft's Web site to get information or technical support. Simply choose Microsoft On The Web from the Help menu, and then choose the appropriate option from the submenu.

Quitting Word

Well, that's it for the basic Word tour. We'll finish up by first showing you several ways to close a document and then how to quit Word:

1. Click the Close button (the one with the X) at the right end of the menu bar (not the title bar) to close Launch Party Letter.

Closing documents

2. When Word asks if you want to save the changes you have made to the document, click Yes.

3. To close the Glacier Bag Party window, use your mouse to choose Close from the File menu and click Yes to save any changes.

4. To close ChillFill Letter, press Alt, then F (the underlined letter in *File* on the menu bar), and then C (the underlined letter in *Close* on the File menu).

5. To quit Word, click the Close button at the right end of the title bar.

Here are some other ways to quit Word:

• Choose Exit from the File menu.

• Press Alt, then F, and then X (the underlined letter in *Exit* on the File menu).

• Double-click the Control menu icon—the W—at the left end of Word's title bar.

2

Letter-Perfect Documents

We produce another document to show how to use the AutoText and AutoCorrect features. We then explore more editing techniques and organize the document in outline view. Finally, we search for and replace text and check spelling.

Assign heading levels and reorganize your documents in outline view

Find and replace text to maintain consistency

Check spelling to avoid embarrassing typos

Use AutoText and AutoCorrect for often-used text

Delete, copy, and move text until it reads exactly right

Glacier Sleeping Bags—Frequently Asked Questions

What is the Glacier Series of sleeping bags?

The Glacier Series was created for use in extreme weather conditions. Glacier sleeping bags are ideal for conditions ranging from 20 degrees Fahrenheit to –30 degrees Fahrenheit. Constructed with quality, rugged materials, Glacier sleeping bags meet the needs of the avid hiker or climber.

Who makes Glacier sleeping bags?

The Glacier Series was designed and manufactured by In The Bag. Founded in 1986 by world-class mountaineer Al Pine, In The Bag has been producing sleeping bags made from high quality materials for ten years. Al Pine, the president of In The Bag, decided to start the company after developing mild hypothermia during a hiking trip in Denali National Park. Among other accolades, In The Bag received the 1992 Rainier Award in Outdoor Product Design for their innovative zipperless Kodiak bags. In The Bag's primary goal is to provide sleeping bags that guarantee a safe, comfortable sleeping atmosphere for people who explore even the farthest corners of the globe.

How are they constructed?

All models of Glacier sleeping bags are made of a durable polyester outer shell that withstands the roughest conditions nature offers. The Glacier 1000 and Glacier 2000 are insulated with ChillFill, an innovative fill made of 100% natural fibers. The Glacier 3000, designed for the coldest weather conditions, uses CozyTec, a new form of insulation created by In The Bag that uses rubber fibers spun from recycled tires as its base. The quilted construction of all three Glacier models ensures that the fill stays evenly distributed for maximum comfort and warmth.

Where are the bags made?

All materials used in Glacier sleeping bags are made in the USA. The bags are assembled in our manufacturing plant in Anchorage, Alaska.

Have the bags been tested in extreme conditions?

In The Bag tests their sleeping bags in their on-site labs and on actual expeditions. In the labs, test dummies are used in simulations of extreme weather conditions, including temperature, precipitation, and wind-chill factors.

How much do they cost?

Prices for Glacier sleeping bags range from $150 to $400. Customized bags cost slightly more. Bulk discounts are available.

How do I order?

You can purchase Glacier sleeping bags in one of three ways: 1. You can buy them at most outdoor equipment stores. 2. You can order them directly from In The Bag by calling 1-800-555-2400 or by faxing us at (907) 555-1451. 3. You can email your order (and/or any further inquiries) to us at custserv@bag.com.

With Word, we can apply fancy formats and add graphics and special effects to increase the impact of a document. But all the frills in the world won't compensate for bad phrasing, bad organization, or errors. That's why this chapter focuses on the Word tools that help us develop and refine the content of our documents. As the example for this chapter, we create a *frequently asked questions page*, or *FAQ*, about In The Bag's new sleeping-bag line. FAQs are often distributed in information packages about a company and are usually included as part of commercial Web sites on the Internet.

First let's enter a few headings to establish the basic structure of the document:

1. Start Word by clicking the Start button and selecting Microsoft Word from the Programs submenu.

2. If necessary, turn off the ruler by choosing Ruler from the View menu. That way, you'll have a bit more room to work.

The Show/Hide ¶ button

3. If necessary, click the Show/Hide ¶ button, to display non-printing characters such as paragraph marks and spaces.

4. Type *What is the Glacier Series of sleeping bags?* and press Enter. Word enters the heading, inserts a paragraph mark, and moves the insertion point to the next line.

5. Type *How are they constructed?* and press Enter.

6. Continue entering the headings shown here (we've magnified the document to make it easier to read):

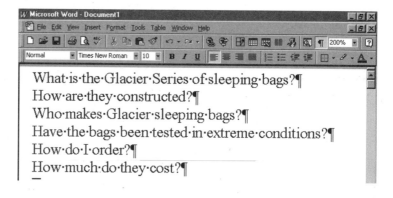

7. Now save the document by clicking the Save button, specifying *Frequently Asked Questions* as the name of the file, and clicking Save.

To get the ball rolling, let's add some text under a heading:

1. Click an insertion point between the question mark and the paragraph mark at the end of the *What is the Glacier Series of sleeping bags?* heading, press Enter, and then type the following text:

The Glacier Series was created for use in extreme weather conditions. Glacier sleeping bags are ideal for conditions ranging from 20 degrees Fahrenheit to -30 degrees Fahrenheit. Constructed with quality, rugged materials, Glacier bags meet the needs of the avid hiker or climber.

We've typed *Glacier* three times. Let's look at a couple of ways we can save keystrokes and ensure that the words and phrases we use repeatedly are always entered correctly.

Storing and Retrieving Often-Used Text

To help us enter often-used text efficiently, accurately, and consistently, Word has two special features: AutoText and AutoCorrect. At first glance these two features seem almost identical; they both enable us to store text or a graphic with a name and then insert the text or graphic in any document at any time simply by typing the name. An AutoText or Auto-Correct entry can be as short as a single text character or as long as several pages of text or graphics. Unlike the contents of the Clipboard, AutoText and AutoCorrect entries are saved from one Word session to the next.

So what's the difference between them? To insert an AutoText entry, we type the entry's name and then press the F3 key. To insert an AutoCorrect entry, we simply type the name; the instant we type a punctuation mark or press the Spacebar, Word automatically replaces the name with its entry.

How do we decide which to use? Here's an example. Suppose we own a landscaping business. We know we'd save a lot of time and effort if we could type *aspen* instead of having to

Web page creation

For the example in this chapter, we create an FAQ page, which as we noted earlier is often used in Web pages. If you plan to publish documents for use on the World Wide Web or on intranets, Word 97 can help you with this process. To turn an existing document into an HTML (HyperText Markup Language) document, simply choose Save As HTML from the File menu. Word saves the file with HTML coding, which formats your document so that it appears in Word the same way it appears in a Web browser. If you know HTML, you can edit the code and text by choosing HTML Source from the View menu. When you finish, click the Exit HTML Source button on the Standard toolbar to return to the formatted version of the document. If you want to create a Web page from scratch, use the Web Page Wizard on the Web Pages tab of the New dialog box.

type and italicize *Populus tremuloides* (the botanical name for the aspen tree) every time we include this tree in a materials list for our wholesaler. But when we communicate with our clients, we want to be able to refer to the aspen tree by its common name rather than its botanical name. This entry is a prime candidate for AutoText because we can control when Word replaces the name *aspen* with the entry *Populus tremuloides* and when it stays plain old *aspen*. If we use AutoCorrect instead, Word will always replace the name *aspen* with *Populus tremuloides*. Let's try both features.

Using AutoText

We use Word's AutoText feature to store text or a graphic so that we can later retrieve it by typing its name and pressing the F3 key. For this example, we'll turn a word we have already typed into an AutoText entry. Follow these steps to simplify the typing of *Glacier*:

Displaying the AutoText toolbar

1. Right-click one of the toolbars and choose AutoText to display the AutoText toolbar.

2. Select *Glacier* in the sentence you just typed and click New on the AutoText toolbar to display this dialog box:

Formatted entries

If you want an AutoText or Auto-Correct entry to retain its paragraph formatting (alignment, indents, and so on), include the paragraph mark when you select the entry. AutoText entries retain their character formatting. If you want an AutoCorrect entry to retain its character formatting, select the Formatted Text option in the AutoCorrect dialog box when you create the entry.

Deleting entries

To delete an AutoText entry, click the AutoText button, select the entry you want to delete from the list, click Delete, and then click OK. To delete an AutoCorrect entry, choose AutoCorrect from the Tools menu, select the entry you want to delete from the list at the bottom of the AutoCorrect dialog box, click Delete, and then click OK.

3. Type *g* in the Please Name Your AutoText Entry edit box and click OK. Word closes the dialog box.

Now let's use the entry we've just created as we write a few more paragraphs for the FAQ:

1. Click an insertion point after the question mark in the *How are they constructed?* paragraph, press Enter, and then type the following (don't press the Spacebar after *g*):

   All models of g

2. Press F3. Word replaces *g* with the *Glacier* entry.

3. Continue typing the following paragraph, using the *g-F3* sequence to insert *Glacier* where indicated. Be sure to type the error marked in bold exactly as you see it so that you will have a mistake to correct later in the chapter. (Word will flag this and any other spelling errors with a red, wavy underline.) Also include the **** characters, which are placeholders for information we'll add later.

   *bags are made of a durable **polester** outer shell that withstands the roughest conditions nature offers. The g-F3 1000 and g-F3 2000 are insulated with ChillFill, an innovative fill made of 100% natural fibers. The g-F3 3000, designed for the coldest weather conditions, uses ****, a new form of insulation created by In The Bag that uses rubber fibers spun from **** as its base. The quilted construction of all three g-F3 models ensures that the fill stays evenly distributed for maximum comfort and warmth.*

   Suppose we forget the code for an AutoText entry. Does that mean we can't use the entry anymore? Not at all. Try this:

1. Click an insertion point at the end of the *How much do they cost?* heading, press Enter, and then type *Prices for* followed by a space.

2. Click the AutoText button on the AutoText toolbar to display the AutoText tab of the AutoCorrect dialog box, shown on the next page.

The AutoText button

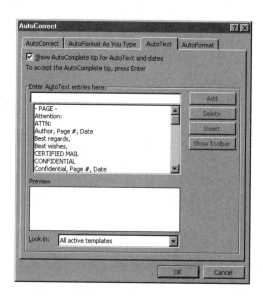

AutoComplete

Included in the list of AutoText entries on the AutoText tab of the AutoCorrect dialog box are AutoComplete entries. All these "autos" may seem a bit confusing, but basically AutoComplete allows you to insert items, such as names, dates, and AutoText entries, by typing only the first few characters of the item. For example, if you type *mond*, a box that displays Monday appears. If Monday is the correct entry, simply press Enter or F3 to insert the word. If Monday is not the correct entry, just ignore it and keep typing. AutoComplete can automatically complete the date, a day of the week, a month, your name, and AutoText entries. To turn off this feature, deselect the Show AutoComplete Tip option on the AutoText tab of the AutoCorrect dialog box. (When AutoComplete is turned off, you need to press F3 to enter any AutoText entries you have created.)

3. Scroll through the list, select *g*, and check the Preview box to see what the entry represents. (The list also includes Auto-Complete entries. See the adjacent tip.) To insert the selected entry, you could click the Insert button, but instead, click OK to close the dialog box, and we'll show you another way to insert the entry.

4. Click the All Entries button on the AutoText toolbar to display a drop-down list of categories of entries, and point to each in turn to see its contents.

5. Select Normal and then *g*. Word inserts the entry *Glacier* at the insertion point.

6. Finish typing the paragraph below:

   bags range from $150 to $400. Bulk discounts are available. Customized bags cost slightly more.

7. Turn off the AutoText toolbar by right-clicking it and selecting AutoText from the object menu.

Now that we've simplified the typing of the word *Glacier*, you've probably noticed other words or phrases that could benefit from the same treatment. How about *In The Bag*? To simplify the typing of this entry, we'll use AutoCorrect.

Using AutoCorrect

We use the AutoCorrect feature when we want Word to automatically replace a name with its entry. AutoCorrect names should be unique sequences of characters that we are not likely to use normally in a document. Try this:

1. In the paragraph that begins *All models of*, select *In The Bag* and then choose AutoCorrect from the Tools menu to display the AutoCorrect tab of the AutoCorrect dialog box:

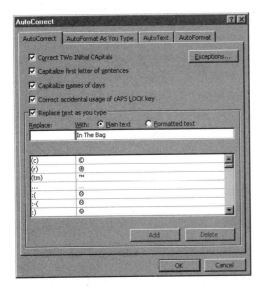

Word is waiting for you to enter the name you want Word to replace with the selected text, which appears in the With edit box. The box below contains a ready-made list of entries for symbols and commonly misspelled words, such as *teh* (the), which Word replaces each time you type them.

← Ready-made AutoCorrect entries

2. In the Replace edit box, type *itb* as the name of the entry and click Add. Word adds the name and its replacement to the list. Then click OK to close the dialog box.

Now let's use this AutoCorrect entry so that you can get a feel for what a time-saver AutoCorrect can be:

1. Click an insertion point at the end of the *Have the bags been tested in extreme conditions?* heading, press Enter, and then type the text shown on the next page.

Bypassing AutoCorrect

To turn off AutoCorrect, deselect the Replace Text As You Type option in the AutoCorrect dialog box. If you don't want to turn off AutoCorrect but you also don't want AutoCorrect to replace a particular instance of a name with its entry, type the name, and after AutoCorrect replaces it, click the Undo button (see page 22).

itb tests their sleeping bags in their on-site labs and on actual expeditions. In the labs, test dummies are used in simulations of extreme weather conditions, including temperature, precipitation, and wind-chill factors.

2. Next, click an insertion point at the end of the *How do I order?* heading, press Enter, and type the following (be sure to misspell *can* as *acn*, one of Word's ready-made AutoCorrect entries):

You acn purchase g-F3 bags in one of three ways: 1. You can buy them at most outdoor equipment stores. 2. You can order them directly from itb by calling 1-800-555-2400 or by faxing us at (907) 555-1451. 3. You can email your order (and/or any further inquiries) to us at custserve@bag.com.

3. Save the document. (From now on, save frequently.)

More Editing Techniques

In Chapter 1, we covered some basic editing techniques that you may have already used in this chapter if you typed any words incorrectly. In this section, we briefly cover some more ways of revising documents. We'll make a few changes to the FAQ to get a feel for what's involved.

More Ways to Delete and Replace Text

Word provides a few techniques for deleting and replacing text in addition to those covered in Chapter 1. We'll learn these techniques as we add a new paragraph to the FAQ:

1. Click an insertion point at the end of the *Who makes Glacier sleeping bags?* heading, press Enter, and type the following (including the errors in bold and the AutoText and Auto-Correct names, which are not italicized):

The g-F3 Series was designed and manufactured by itb. Founded in 1985 by world-class mountaineer Al Pine, itb has been producing outdoor sleeping bags made from high quality materials for ten years. Al Pine, teh current president of itb, decided to start teh company after developing mild **hypothemia** *during a hiking trip in Denali National Park. Among other accolades, itb received the 1992 Rainier Award*

AutoCorrect options

In the AutoCorrect dialog box are several options that take care of common typing "errors." Word can correct two initial capital letters in a word, correct sentences that don't begin with a capital letter, capitalize the days of the week, and correct accidental usage of the Caps Lock key. You can turn any of these options on or off by clicking the corresponding check box. If you click the Exceptions button, you can tell Word not to capitalize the word immediately following an abbreviation (such as *apt.* for *apartment*). Or you can tell Word not to correct two consecutive initial capital letters in certain instances.

in Outdoor Product Design for their innovative zipperless Kodiak bags. itb*'s primary goal is to provide sleeping bags that guarantee a safe,* **comforatable** *sleeping atmosphere for people who explore even* teh *furthest corners of the globe.*

2. Click an insertion point to the right of the *r* in *outdoor* (in the second sentence) and then press Ctrl+Backspace to delete the word to the left of the insertion point.

3. Now, click an insertion point to the left of the *c* in *current* (in the third sentence) and press Ctrl+Delete to delete the word to the right of the insertion point.

As you have seen, Word is by default in Insert mode. When we click an insertion point and begin typing, the characters we enter are inserted to the left of the insertion point, pushing any existing text to the right. Word can also operate in Overtype mode, so that when we click an insertion point and begin typing, each character we enter replaces an existing character.

← Insert mode

← Overtype mode

Let's experiment a bit with overtyping. Suppose In The Bag was actually founded in 1986, not 1985. Here's how to make this simple correction:

1. Click an insertion point between the *8* and *5* of *1985* under the *Who makes Glacier sleeping bags?* heading.

2. In the status bar, double-click the Overtype box (the fourth box from the right, which contains the letters *OVR*). The letters *OVR* are highlighted to indicate that you are now in Overtype mode.

3. Type *6*, which overtypes the 5, so that the entry now correctly reads *1986*.

4. Double-click the Overtype box to turn off Overtype mode. This step is important; you might overtype valuable information if you forget it.

More Ways to Move and Copy Text

As you saw in Chapter 1, we can move any amount of text within the same document or to a different document. Move operations can either be carried out using the Cut and Paste

Tracking editing changes

To keep track of editing changes, you can use tools available on the Reviewing toolbar. (Right-click a toolbar and select Reviewing from the object menu to display this toolbar.) Click the Track Changes button to display revisions underlined and in red. The letters *TRK* in the status bar indicate you are in track changes mode. (To adjust the display of revisions, choose Options from the Tools menu and change the settings on the Track Changes tab.) You can insert comments using the Insert Comment button and save the document with comments using the Save Version button. To stop tracking changes, you can either click the Track Changes button on the Reviewing toolbar or double-click the letters *TRK* in the status bar.

Drag-and-drop editing → buttons as discussed in Chapter 1 or by using a mouse technique called *drag-and-drop editing*. Generally, we use drag-and-drop editing when moving text short distances—that is, when the text we're moving and its destination can be viewed simultaneously. Try this:

Moving text with drag-and-drop editing →

1. Select the sentence that begins *Bulk discounts* under the *How much do they cost?* heading.

2. Point to the highlighted text, hold down the left mouse button, drag the shadow insertion point after the last period in the paragraph, and release the mouse button. The selected text moves to the specified location. You have, in effect, transposed the last two sentences in this paragraph.

3. Press End and then press Enter to add a new, blank paragraph at the end of the document.

4. Select the *How do I order?* heading and the following paragraph and then drag-and-drop them below the *How much do they cost?* heading.

The procedure for copying text is similar to that for moving text. Try copying some text with the drag-and-drop technique:

1. Press Ctrl+Home to move to the top of the document.

Copying text with drag-and-drop editing →

2. Click an insertion point at the beginning of the sentence that reads *The Glacier Series* under the *Who makes Glacier sleeping bags?* heading.

No automatic replacement

You can have Word insert what you type to the left of a selection instead of replacing it. Choose Options from the Tools menu, and click the Edit tab to display the editing options. Then simply click the Typing Replaces Selection option to deselect it, and click OK.

Smart editing

When you cut or copy and paste text, Word intuits where spaces are needed in the text. For example, it usually removes spaces before or adds them after punctuation marks. To tell Word to leave these adjustments to you, choose Options from the Tools menu, click the Edit tab, click the Use Smart Cut And Paste option to deselect it, and click OK.

Drag-and-drop problems

If pointing to a text selection and then holding down the mouse button does not move the text but instead deselects the text and creates an insertion point, the Drag-And-Drop Text Editing option is turned off. To turn it on, choose Options from the Tools menu, click the Edit tab, select the option, and then click OK.

3. Select the sentence by holding down Ctrl and Shift simultaneously and then pressing the Right Arrow key until you have highlighted the entire sentence.

4. Point to the selected text, hold down the left mouse button, and drag the shadow insertion point to the right of the last period in the document's first paragraph (after *climber*). While still holding down the mouse button, hold down the Ctrl key (a small plus sign appears next to the mouse pointer), and then release the key and the mouse button together. Immediately, a copy of the selected sentence appears in the location designated by the shadow insertion point, as shown here:

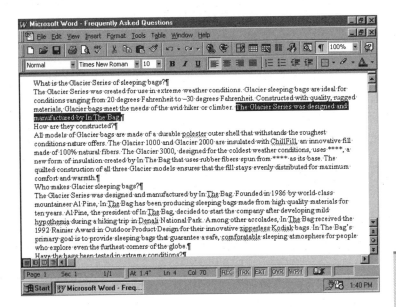

5. With the sentence you just copied still selected, press Delete.

Organizing Documents

We have seen how to move text around in a document using cut-and-paste and drag-and-drop editing, but when a document has headings as well as ordinary text, it's often simpler to use Word's Outlining feature to move things around. Most people are accustomed to thinking of outlining as the process that precedes the writing of lengthy documents. With Word, however, outlining is not a separate process but simply another way of looking at a document. If all we ever do is write

Extend-selection mode

You can use extend-selection mode as another way to select text. Click an insertion point where you want the selection to start and then turn on extend-selection mode by pressing F8 or double-clicking the letters *EXT* in the status bar. Then click where you want the selection to end, and Word immediately highlights all the text between the insertion point and the spot where you clicked. To turn off extend-selection mode, simply press Esc or double-click the letters *EXT* in the status bar.

letters, memos, and other short documents, we may never use outlining. But if we write longer documents with headings, such as business plans, company reports, or term papers, outlining provides a powerful way of quickly organizing and reorganizing our information. Once we use Word's Outlining feature with a particular document, we can switch to outline view at any time to get an overview of our work.

In this section, we'll set up the outline for the FAQ and then use it to reorganize the document. Let's get started:

1. Choose Outline from the View menu. Word displays the Outlining toolbar, which allows you to organize your document by assigning levels to the information on the screen. Because Word considers all the headings and paragraphs of the FAQ to be ordinary body text, each one is identified in the selection area to its left by a small hollow square.

2. Move the pointer over the Outlining toolbar, using ToolTips to get an idea of what each button does, and then press Ctrl+End to move to the end of the document.

The Promote button

Heading styles

3. On a new line, type *Glacier Sleeping Bags- -Frequently Asked Questions*, and then click the Promote button on the Outlining toolbar. Word moves the heading to the left and makes it bigger to reflect its new status. (Word has also replaced the two hyphens you typed with an em dash.) Notice that Heading 1, the style that Word has applied to the heading, appears in the Style box at the left end of the Formatting toolbar. (See page 73 for more information about styles.) With Word, you can create up to nine heading levels, called Heading 1 through Heading 9. Also notice the large minus button next to the heading; it indicates that the heading has no subheadings or text.

4. Click an insertion point in the *How do I order?* heading and click the Promote button. Repeat this step for each of the remaining five headings to change them to the Heading 1 style.

The Show Heading 1 button

5. Click the Show Heading 1 button. Word collapses the outline so that only the level 1 headings are visible:

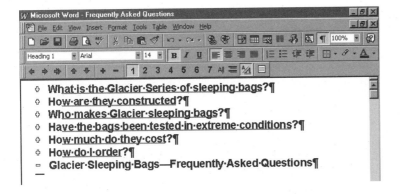

As we've already mentioned, a minus button indicates that the heading doesn't have subordinate headings or text; a plus button indicates that it does. In addition, Word puts a gray underline below headings whose subordinate information is hidden in this mode.

Outline symbols

Now let's do a little reorganizing:

1. Click anywhere in the *Glacier Sleeping Bags—Frequently Asked Questions* heading and click the Move Up button repeatedly until the heading is at the top of the document.

The Move Up button

2. Click an insertion point in the *How are they constructed?* heading and then click the Move Down button once to move the heading below the *Who makes Glacier sleeping bags?* heading.

The Move Down button

Using the document map

Another way to view your Word documents is by using the document map. Click the Document Map button on the Standard toolbar to display the document map, which contains all of the headings of the document, in a separate pane on the left side of the screen. To move to a different heading, click the heading in the document map pane. That heading moves to the top of the page in the pane on the right. To change the level of display in the document map, click a minus sign to collapse subheadings under a main heading. To redisplay subheadings, click a plus sign. For more specific levels of display, right-click a heading and choose an option from the object menu. To resize the document map pane, move the pointer to the dividing line between the left and right panes, and when the pointer changes to a double-headed arrow, drag in the appropriate direction. To close the document map, either click the Document Map button or double-click the dividing line between the left and right panes.

Deleting headings

To delete a heading from an outline, select the heading and press Delete. If you want to also delete the heading's subordinate headings and text, collapse the outline before you make your selection. Otherwise, expand the outline before you select the heading so that you can see exactly which paragraphs will be affected when you press Delete.

The Expand button

3. Click the Expand button to display the body text below the selected heading. As you can see here, the paragraph moved with its heading:

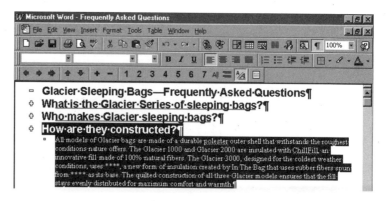

The Collapse button

4. Click the Collapse button to hide the text again.

What happens if we want to add information to the document while we are in outline view? Simple! Follow these steps:

1. Click an insertion point at the end of the *How are they constructed?* heading and press Enter. Word assumes you want to type another level 1 heading.

2. Type *Where are the bags made?* and press Enter.

The Demote To Body Text button

3. Click the Demote To Body Text button on the Outlining toolbar and type the following, including the errors in bold:

*All **materiuls** used in g-F3 bags are made in the USA. The bags are assembled in our **manufacuring** plant in Anchorage, Alaska.*

4. Click the Show Heading 1 button to display only the headings.

Notice that all the headings except the first should really be level 2. You have used the Promote button to bump headings up one level. Here's how to bump them down:

The Demote button

1. Select all the headings except the first and then click the Demote button on the Outlining toolbar. Word both changes their formatting and moves the selected headings to the right so that their relationship to the level 1 heading above is readily apparent. In the Style box on the Formatting toolbar, Heading

2 is displayed. The minus icon to the left of the first heading changes to a plus icon, indicating that it now has subordinate headings and text.

2. Click the Show All button to see these results:

The Show All button

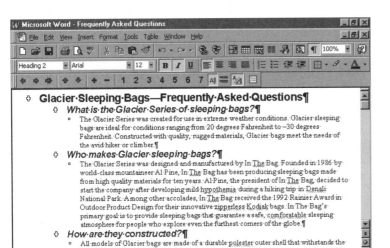

Well, after that brief introduction to Word's Outlining feature, we'll return to normal view so that we can move on with the rest of the chapter:

1. Click the Normal View button at the left end of the horizontal scroll bar. Having set up the document's outline, you can return to outline view at any time by simply clicking the Outline View button at the left end of the horizontal scroll bar.

The Normal View and Outline View buttons

2. Click the Save button to save your work.

Finding and Replacing

With Word, we can search a document for specific characters. We can also specify replacement characters. As you'll see if you follow along with the next example, finding a series of characters is easy.

Finding Text

Recall that while typing the Glacier sleeping bag FAQ, we left the characters **** as placeholders for information that needed to be added later. Suppose we now need to locate the

Editing during a search or replace

To edit a document without closing the Find And Replace dialog box, click the document window to activate it, make your changes, and then click anywhere in the Find And Replace dialog box to continue the search or replace. You can also click the Cancel button to close the Find And Replace dialog box and instead use the Next Find/Go To and Previous Find/ Go To buttons at the bottom of the vertical scroll bar to complete your search without the dialog box in your way.

placeholders so that we can substitute the correct information. In a document as short as the FAQ, we would have no difficulty locating ****. But if the current document were many pages long and several placeholders were involved, we would probably want to use the Find command to locate them. Follow these steps:

The Find command

1. Press Ctrl+Home to move the insertion point to the top of the document.

2. Choose Find from the Edit menu. Word displays the dialog box shown here:

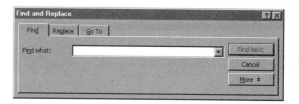

3. Enter **** in the Find What edit box and click Find Next. Word searches the document, stopping when it locates the first occurrence of ****.

4. Click Cancel to close the dialog box and then type *CozyTec* to replace the highlighted placeholder.

The Next Find/Go To and Previous Find/Go To buttons

5. Click the Next Find/Go To button at the bottom of the vertical scroll bar to repeat the Find command using the same Find What text as the previous search. Word locates the second ****. (You can click the Previous Find/Go To button to go back to the previous instance of the Find What text.)

6. Replace the selection with *recycled tires*.

Most of our searches will be as simple as this one was, but we can also refine our searches by first clicking the More button in the Find And Replace dialog box to display additional options. We can then use these options or enter special characters (see the tip on page 48). For example, suppose we regularly confuse the two words *further* and *farther*. We can check our use of these words in the FAQ, as follows:

1. Press Ctrl+Home to move to the top of the document. Then click the Select Browse Object button at the bottom of the vertical scroll bar to display this palette of options:

The Select Browse Object button

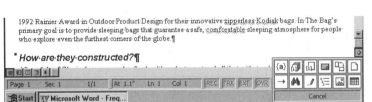

These buttons allow you to browse through your document by heading, graphic, table and so on.

2. Click the Find button to display the Find And Replace dialog box again.

The Find button

3. Next, click the More button to expand the Find And Replace dialog box, as shown here:

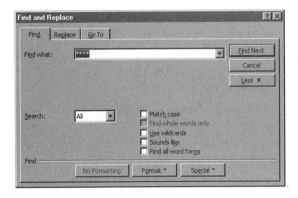

4. Enter *f?rthe* in the Find What edit box. The ? is a *wildcard* character that stands for any single character.

5. Check that All is selected as the Search option. Then click Use Wildcards to tell Word to look for a string of characters that matches the Find What text, and click Find Next to start the search. Word stops at the word *furthest* in the second paragraph. (You may need to move the dialog box by dragging its title bar so that you can see the text.)

Finding and replacing formats

To search for text with an assigned format, choose Find from the Edit menu, click the More button to expand the Find And Replace dialog box, click the Format button, and then click Font (for character formats) or Paragraph. In the Find Font or Find Paragraph dialog box, specify the format you seek, click OK to return to the Find And Replace dialog box, and click Find Next. Word highlights the next text entry with the assigned format. You can use the Replace command to change a particular format. For example, to change all bold text to bold italic, choose Replace from the Edit menu, click Format and then Font, click Bold in the Font Style list, and click OK. Then click the Replace With edit box, click Format and then Font, click Bold Italic in the Font Style list, and click OK. Back in the Find And Replace dialog box, click Find Next and Replace, if you want to confirm each change of the specified format, or click Replace All.

6. This use of *furthest* is incorrect, so click Cancel to close the dialog box and change the *u* to *a*.

7. Click the Next Find/Go To button to repeat the search. Word stops at the word *further*, which is correct.

8. Click the Next Find/Go To button again to ensure that the document contains no other instances of the Find What text, and click No when Word asks whether you want to continue the search.

Replacing Text

Often, we will search a document for a series of characters with the intention of replacing them. When we need to make the same replacement more than a couple of times, using the Replace command automates the process. As an example, let's find all occurrences of *Glacier bags* and change them to *Glacier sleeping bags*:

1. Press Ctrl+Home to move to the beginning of the document, click the Select Browse Object button, click Find, and click the Replace tab.(You can also use the Replace command on the Edit menu.) Word displays the dialog box shown here:

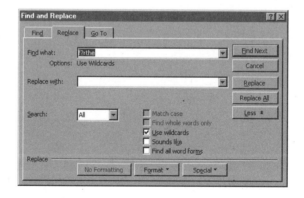

Notice that the text and settings from the last search have been retained.

2. Replace the Find What text by typing *Glacier bags*.

Refining your searches

By using the options available in the Find And Replace dialog box, you can complete more complicated searches in your Word documents. Use the drop-down list of Search options to search forward (Down) or backward (Up) from the insertion point, or to search the entire document (All). Click the Match Case option to find only those occurrences of the Find What text with the exact capitalization specified. For example, find the initials *USA* and not the characters *usa* in *usability*. Click the Find Whole Words Only option to find only whole-word occurrences of the Find What text. For example, find the word *men* and not the characters *men* in *fundamental*. Find special characters, such as tabs and paragraph marks, by selecting them from the Special drop-down list. For example, find the paragraphs that begin with *Remember* by selecting Paragraph Mark from the list and then typing *Remember* after ^p as the Find What text. Click the Sounds Like option to find occurrences of the Find What text that sound the same but are spelled differently. Finally, click the Find All Word Forms option to find occurrences of a particular word in any form. For example, if the Find What text is the word *hide*, Word will also find *hid* and *hidden*.

3. In the Replace With edit box, type *Glacier sleeping bags.* Click the Less button to decrease the size of the dialog box, and press Enter. Word highlights the first occurrence of the Find What text.

4. Click Replace. Word continues the search and highlights the second occurrence.

5. Click Replace All to replace any remaining occurrences, and then click OK when Word tells you that four replacements have been made.

6. Click Close to close the Find And Replace dialog box.

As with the Find command, we can use the Match Case, Find Whole Words Only, Use Wildcards, Sounds Like, and Find All Word Forms options to refine the replace procedure. (See the tip on the facing page for more information.)

Checking Spelling

Nothing detracts from a document like a typo. In the past, our readers might have overlooked the occasional misspelling. These days, running a word processor's spelling checker is so easy that readers tend to be less forgiving. For example, resumés and job-application letters with typos will often end up in the recycling bin. The moral: We should get in the habit of spell-checking all our documents, especially before distributing printed copies.

As we created the FAQ in this chapter, we deliberately included a few errors. By default, Word checks the spelling of each word we type against its built-in dictionary and flags any word it does not find with a red, wavy underline. It also checks for grammatical errors, flagging them with a green, wavy underline. These features, called *automatic spell checking* and *automatic grammar checking*, can be turned on or off by clicking the Check Spelling As You Type and Check Grammar As You Type check boxes on the Spelling & Grammar tab of the Options dialog box.

Checking grammar

As we've said, when automatic grammar checking is turned on, Word works behind the scenes, checking your grammar as you type and underlining suspicious phrases with green, wavy underlines. Right-clicking underlined phrases displays a dialog box with suggested changes. The usefulness of the grammar checker depends on the complexity of your writing. Only you can decide whether its suggestions are valid and helpful enough to warrant leaving it turned on. If you want to spell-check your documents without using Word's Grammar checker, deselect the Check Grammar As You Type and Check Grammar With Spelling options at the bottom of the Spelling & Grammar tab.

Usually we will want to correct any errors Word identifies as we go along. Let's try fixing one of the misspelled words now. Follow these steps:

1. Point to the word *hypothemia* in the second body-text paragraph of the FAQ and right-click it. Word displays the object menu shown here:

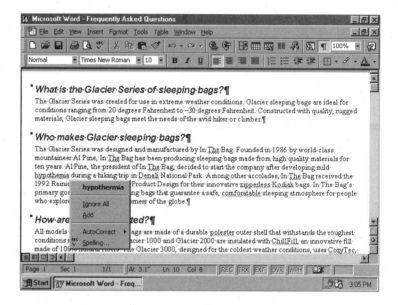

Word displays any words in its dictionary that come close to the offending text. It also gives you the options of ignoring the misspelling, adding the word to a supplemental dictionary, creating an AutoCorrect entry for the word, or displaying the Spelling & Grammar dialog box, which offers more options.

2. Click *hypothermia* to change the word to its correct spelling.

If we prefer to check the spelling of a document all at once, we can use Word's spell-checking capabilities in another way. Follow these steps:

1. Press Ctrl+Home to move to the top of the FAQ, and click the Spelling And Grammar button on the toolbar. Word automat-

The Spelling And Grammar button

ically begins checking each word of the document, starting with the word containing the insertion point, against its built-in dictionary. When it finds a word that is not in its dictionary, Word highlights the word and displays this Spelling And Grammar dialog box:

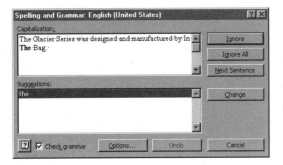

2. As you can see, Word stopped at the word *The* in the company name, suggesting that we lowercase the word. Since it is part of the company name, click the Ignore All button to tell Word that you want to ignore all occurrences of this grammar problem. (The green, wavy underline disappears from the word throughout the document.)

3. Next, Word stops on the word *Denali*. Possible substitutes appear in the Suggestions list. Since this spelling is correct, click Ignore All. (The red, wavy underline disappears from every occurrence of the word.)

4. Word stops at the word *zipperless*. Although this term is not in Word's dictionary, it is correct, so click Ignore All again.

5. Word stops at *Kodiak,* which is the name of a sleeping-bag type (as well as the name of a geographical region and a bear), so click Ignore All.

6. Next, Word questions *comforatable*—a genuine misspelling. Click Change to accept Word's suggestion, *comfortable*.

Spelling and grammar options

Clicking the Options button in the Spelling And Grammar dialog box displays the Spelling & Grammar tab (like the Spelling & Grammar tab in the Options dialog box). Here you can tell Word whether you want it to automatically spell- and grammar-check the current document or hide error notification in the document. You can also tell Word to suggest alternatives for the misspellings it finds and to ignore words in capital letters or that contain numbers. In addition, you can create, edit, add, and delete custom dictionaries by clicking the Dictionaries button (see page 53).

7. Word comes to *polester* and suggests *pollster*. Click *polyester* in the Suggestions list and then click Change.

8. Next, Word stops on *ChillFill*. You have spelled this name correctly and use it often. To prevent Word from flagging it as a misspelling every time, add it to Word's supplemental dictionary, Custom.dic, by clicking the Add button. (You cannot add words to the main dictionary.) Repeat this procedure to add *CozyTec* to the supplemental dictionary.

9. As Word continues the spell check, change *materiuls* to *materials* and *manufacuring* to *manufacturing*.

10. When Word reaches the end of the document, it closes the Spelling And Grammar dialog box and displays a message that the spelling and grammar check is complete. Click OK to return to your document.

11. Save and then close the document. (We will use it again in Chapter 3.)

As you create documents and spell-check them, you will start to see that the words you use fall into several categories:

- Common words that are included in Word's main dictionary.

- Uncommon words that you use rarely. You will want to tell Word to ignore these words when spell-checking a document. Word will then attach those words to the document in which they are used as a sort of document-specific dictionary and will not flag them as misspellings if you spell-check the document in the future.

- Uncommon words that you use often in different kinds of documents. You will want to add these words to Custom.dic so that they are not flagged as misspellings.

- Uncommon words that you use with a specific type of document. Instead of adding these words to Custom.dic, you might want to create a custom dictionary for use only with that type

Smart spelling checks

If your document contains duplicate words, such as *the the*, Word stops at the words and displays them in the Spelling And Grammar dialog box during a spelling check. Clicking Delete removes the duplicate word. To speed up the checking process, Word's suggestions generally have the same case as a misspelled word. For example, if the misspelling occurs at the beginning of a sentence and therefore starts with a capital letter, Word's suggestions also start with capital letters.

of document. To create a custom dictionary, choose Options from the Tools menu, click the Spelling & Grammar tab, click the Dictionaries button, and then click the New button in the Custom Dictionaries dialog box. Type a name for the dictionary, click Save, and then click OK. Before you can use the custom dictionary, you must open it by selecting it from the drop-down list in the Options dialog box and clicking OK. (You can also create and open custom dictionaries on the Spelling & Grammar tab that appears when you click Options in the Spelling And Grammar dialog box.) Then when you check a document's spelling, you can click the Add button in the Spelling And Grammar dialog box to add words to the custom dictionary. (Before starting a spelling check, it is a good idea to click the Options button and check which custom dictionary is in effect.)

We can't rely on Word's spelling and grammar checker to identify every error in our documents. Errors of syntax or improper word usage can easily slip by in a spelling and grammar check. We should always read through our documents to look for any errors that Word might miss.

← Creating custom dictionaries

The Thesaurus

You can use the Word Thesaurus to look up synonyms for a selected word by choosing Language and then Thesaurus from the Tools menu. Word displays the Thesaurus dialog box and suggests alternative words for the selected word. To replace the word in your document with one of these alternatives, select the new word in the Replace With Synonym list and click the Replace button. You can also select an alternative word and click Look Up to display a list of alternatives for the alternative! Click Cancel to close the Thesaurus dialog box without making any changes.

3 Eye-Catching Documents

We create a memo and a fax by exploring Word's built-in templates and wizards. Then we combine two documents to demonstrate some of Word's formatting capabilities, including multiple columns, lists, and styles.

Use a template to create an impressive memo

Use a wizard to create a professional-looking fax

Dress up headings with borders and shading

In The Bag

Memo

To:

From:

CC:

Date:

Re:

New Gl

In The Ba
complete
finished a
unique ar
temperatu

A launch
developm
about the

● Page 1

1200 Yukon Ave.
Anchorage, AK 99502
Phone: 907-555-1450
Fax: 907-555-1451

In The Bag

Fax

To:

Fax:

Phone:

Re:

☐ Urgen

In The Ba
complete
finished a
unique ar
temperatu

A launch
developm
about the

New Glacier Sleeping Bags Ideal for Extreme Conditions

In The Bag is pleased to announce that the **Glacier Series**, our latest line of sleeping bags, is now complete and ready for production. Thanks to the hard work of our development team, the product was finished ahead of schedule. The use of ChillFill insulation is instrumental in making Glacier bags so unique and exciting. Many retail stores have already placed large orders for these innovative, subzero-temperature sleeping bags.

A launch party will be held on Saturday, June 21, 1997 to honor those who contributed to the development of this excellent line. In The Bag's President, Al Pine, will be on hand to answer questions about the Glacier Series.

GLACIER SLEEPING BAGS—FREQUENTLY ASKED QUESTIONS

What is the Glacier Series of sleeping bags?

The Glacier Series was created for use in extreme weather conditions. Glacier sleeping bags are ideal for conditions ranging from 20 degrees Fahrenheit to –30 degrees Fahrenheit. Constructed with quality, rugged materials, Glacier sleeping bags meet the needs of the avid hiker or climber.

Who makes Glacier sleeping bags?

The Glacier Series was designed and manufactured by In The Bag. Founded in 1986 by world-class mountaineer Al Pine, In The Bag has been producing sleeping bags made from high quality materials for ten years. Al Pine, the president of In The Bag, decided to start the company after developing mild hypothermia during a hiking trip in Denali National Park. Among other accolades, In The Bag received the 1992 Rainier Award in Outdoor Product Design for their innovative zipperless Kodiak bags. In The Bag's primary goal is to provide sleeping bags that guarantee a safe,

comfortable sleeping atmosphere for people who explore even the farthest corners of the globe.

How are they constructed?

All models of Glacier sleeping bags are made of a durable polyester outer shell that withstands the roughest conditions nature offers. The Glacier 1000 and Glacier 2000 are insulated with ChillFill, an innovative fill made of 100% natural fibers. The Glacier 3000, designed for the coldest weather conditions, uses CozyTec, a new form of insulation created by In The Bag that uses rubber fibers spun from recycled tires as its base. The quilted construction of all three Glacier models ensures that the fill stays evenly distributed for maximum comfort and warmth.

Where are the bags made?

All materials used in Glacier sleeping bags are made in the USA. The bags are assembled in our manufacturing plant in Anchorage, Alaska.

Have the bags been tested in extreme conditions?

In The Bag tests their sleeping bags in their on-site labs and on actual expeditions. In the labs, test dummies are used in simulations of extreme weather conditions, including temperature, precipitation, and wind-chill factors.

How much do they cost?

Prices for Glacier sleeping bags range from $150 to $400. Customized bags cost slightly more. Bulk discounts are available.

How do I order?

You can purchase Glacier sleeping bags in one of three ways:

1. You can buy them at most outdoor equipment stores.
2. You can order them directly from In The Bag by calling 1-800-555-2400 or by faxing us at (907) 555-1451.
3. You can email your order (and/or any further inquiries) to us at custserv@bag.com.

Set off paragraphs with first line indents and space above and below

Use multicolumn formats to vary document design

Use autoformatting to quickly create numbered and bulleted lists

Turn formatting combinations into styles

This chapter focuses on ways to produce documents with eye-appeal. We start by exploring Word's ready-made templates and wizards, which enable us to quickly create professional-looking documents without having to fuss with formatting. Then we discuss the Word capabilities that enable us to give all our documents that professional touch.

Using Word's Templates

A template is a pattern that includes the information, formatting, and other elements used in a particular type of document. Unless we specify otherwise, all new Word documents are based on the Blank Document template. Word comes with several other templates that we can use as is or modify; or we can create our own templates (see the tip on page 59, and page 96).

As part of the Microsoft Word installation procedure, Word's templates were copied to the Templates subfolder of the Program Files/Microsoft Office folder on your hard drive. To preview these templates, follow these steps:

1. Start Word by clicking the Start button and choosing Programs and then Microsoft Word from the Start menu.

2. Check that both the ruler (choose Ruler from the View menu) and nonprinting characters (click the Show/Hide ¶ button) are displayed.

3. Choose New from the File menu to display this multi-tabbed dialog box:

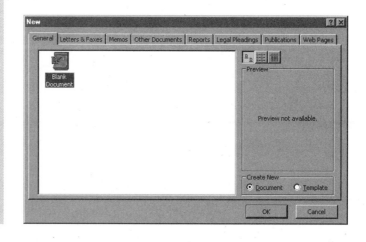

Installing templates

Depending on the type of setup you selected, you may or may not have included all of Word's templates when you installed Word on your computer. To install the templates, close any open applications (including the Office shortcut bar if you are using Microsoft Office), and choose Settings and then Control Panel from the Start menu. Double-click the Add/Remove Programs icon in the Control Panel window and click the Install button on the Install/Uninstall tab. When the first Install Wizard dialog box appears, follow the instructions and click Next. The wizard searches your floppy drive and CD-ROM drive for an installation program and enters the program's pathname in its final dialog box. Click Finish to display the Setup dialog box, and then click the Add/Remove button. Select Wizards And Templates (if you're using Microsoft Office, you will have to select Microsoft Word first) and click the Change Option button. Select More Wizards, click OK twice, and then click Continue to proceed with the installation.

Word separates the templates into categories on different tabs. The default selection (which is available even when the other templates haven't been installed) is Blank Document on the General tab.

4. Click the Letters & Faxes tab and click the Fax Wizard once to highlight it. The Preview box on the right side of the dialog box displays a preview of the highlighted item.

Previewing templates

5. Click more templates on the Letters & Faxes tab and then switch to some of the other tabs. As you can tell from their names and previews, the templates provide the basis for many common business documents.

6. When you are ready, select Professional Memo on the Memos tab, and either press Enter or click OK. Word switches to page layout view and displays this memo form on your screen:

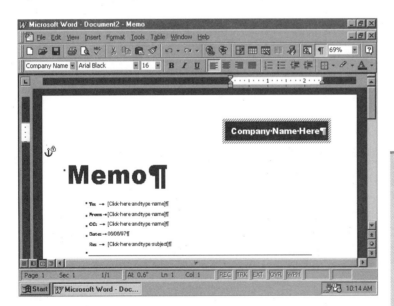

As you can see, all the common elements of a memo have placeholders within square brackets, and Word has entered the current date (using the date stored in your computer—see the tip on the next page). Let's fill in the memo now:

1. In the black box on the right, select *Company Name Here* but not the paragraph mark, and replace it by typing *In The Bag*.

Page layout view

Page layout view is a cross between normal view and print preview. To use it, click the Page Layout View button at the left end of the horizontal scroll bar. In this view, you can see the layout of your pages at a size that allows efficient editing and formatting. For example, the pages appear with margins, headers, and footers visible on the screen. When working with longer documents that contain lots of formatting and graphics, you may find that working in page layout view slows down your computer.

(If you ax a paragraph mark by mistake, immediately click the Undo button on the toolbar to reinstate it.)

2. In the To section, click the placeholder text to select it and its square brackets, and type *Kara Boo*.

3. In the From section, type *Ida Down*, and in the CC: section, type *Chip Monk*.

4. Finally, in the Re: section, type *Glacier Bag Launch Party*.

5. Now select the title *How to Use This Memo Template* but not the paragraph mark, and replace it with *New Glacier Sleeping Bags Ideal for Extreme Conditions.*

Take a moment to admire your work. Without adding any formatting of your own, you've created a professional-looking header for a memo, as shown here:

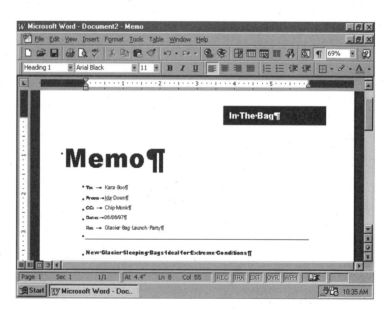

6. Choose Save As from the File menu and save the document with the name *Glacier Memo*.

Below the memo title, we need to enter the text of the memo. This information is essentially the same as that contained in the letter we wrote in Chapter 1. The beauty of a word

Date fields

Word automatically enters the date stored by your system's clock/ calendar when you open a document based on the memo template. Why? Because the document contains a special code called a *field*. Fields can contain a variety of information; this particular field instructs Word to get the current date and display it in the field's location. If you do nothing to this field, Word will insert the current date each time you open the document. If you want to "freeze" the current date, click the field to select it, and press Ctrl+Shift+F9. The field is converted to normal text that will not be updated and that can be edited. To insert a date field in a document, choose Date And Time from the Insert menu, and in the Date And Time dialog box, select a date format, click the Update Automatically option to select it, and click OK.

processor like Word is that instead of retyping the information, we can borrow it from the letter and edit it to suit the purpose of the memo. Here's how:

1. Select the text of the main paragraph (but not the paragraph mark) and press the Delete key.

2. To open the letter from Chapter 1 in its own window, click the Open button on the toolbar, and in the Open dialog box, double-click Launch Party Letter.

3. Select the two main paragraphs of the letter, including the paragraph mark between them, and click the Copy button.

4. Choose Glacier Memo from the bottom of the Window menu and press Ctrl+End to make sure the insertion point is in the blank paragraph at the end of the memo.

5. Click the Paste button to insert the copied text.

6. Edit the text of the memo so that it looks like the one shown below. (We've magnified the memo so that the text is more readable.)

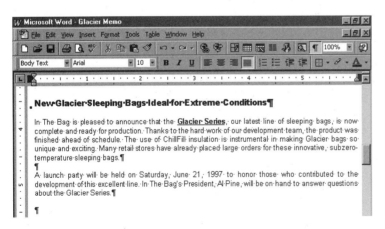

7. Print and save the document, and then close it.

8. Close Launch Party Letter, clicking No if Word asks whether you want to save any changes.

Creating custom templates

You can save any document as a template for future use. Choose Save As from the File menu, click the down arrow to the right of the Save As Type box, and select Document Template. Word displays the contents of the Templates subfolder. Double-click the folder in which you want to store the new template. Assign its name in the File Name edit box and click Save. To use the new template, choose New from the File menu and select the template the same way you would select any of Word's templates.

Using Word's Wizards

When we create a new document based on a wizard, the wizard makes multiple—and often complex—decisions based on our answers to its questions. Let's use the Fax Wizard to create a fax to announce In The Bag's new line of Glacier sleeping bags:

Creating a fax

1. Choose New from the File menu, click the Letters & Faxes tab, and double-click Fax Wizard to display the wizard's first dialog box:

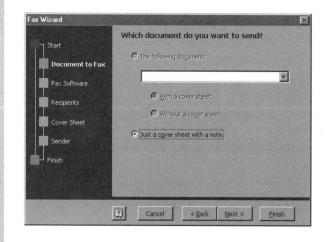

Wizards

Wizards are tools that are incorporated into Word to help you accomplish specific tasks. They all work in the same basic way, regardless of the task. Each consists of a series of dialog boxes asking you to provide information or to select from various options. You move from box to box by clicking the Next button, and you can move back to an earlier box by clicking the Back button. Clicking Cancel aborts the entire procedure. Clicking Finish tells the wizard to complete the task with the current settings. Some wizards, like the Fax Wizard, include a "road map" with colored boxes representing the wizard's steps. You can see exactly where you are in the process by glancing at the boxes, and you can jump to a particular step by clicking its box.

2. Click Next to display the second dialog box:

3. Be sure the Just A Cover Sheet With A Note option is selected and then click Next to display the wizard's third dialog box:

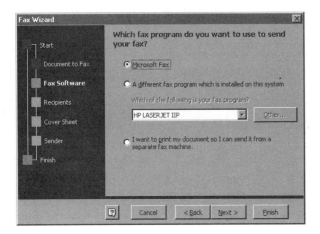

4. Click the third option so that you can print out the document and send it from a separate fax machine. Then click Next to display this dialog box:

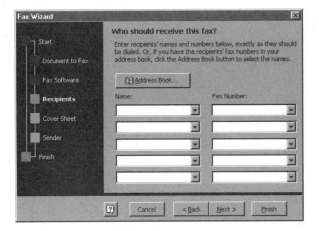

Here, you can select names and numbers from an electronic address book (see page 145 for more information about this feature), or you can type in the names and numbers manually. (If the Fax Wizard has been used before, the names of recent fax recipients may appear in the drop-down lists.)

More Fax Wizard options

If you plan to send a fax to several people at once, you can do so using the Fax Wizard. Simply fill in the names and numbers in the fourth dialog box (or use an electronic address book—see page 145 for more information). After you've completed all of the wizard's dialog boxes, Word displays the fax along with the Mail Merge toolbar. The names and numbers you included are now merge fields. To view the fields, click the View Merged Data button on the Mail Merge toolbar and then cycle through the faxes by clicking the Next Record or Previous Record button. To print the faxes, click the Merge To Printer button on the Mail Merge toolbar. (We discuss the topic of mail merge more in Chapter 6.) To send faxes directly from your computer, you must have a modem connected and turned on. Select your fax program in the third Fax Wizard dialog box. (Microsoft Fax comes with Windows 95.) When Word displays your fax, you can complete the document and click the Send Fax Now button on the Fax Wizard toolbar. Word then walks you through the steps for sending your fax.

5. With the insertion point located in the top Name box, type *Fern Leaf*, press Tab, type *907-555-1201*, and click Next to display the dialog box shown here:

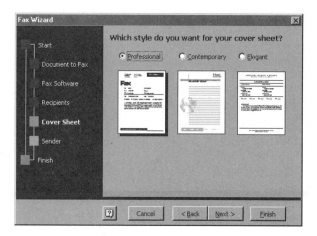

6. With the Professional option selected, click Next to display this dialog box:

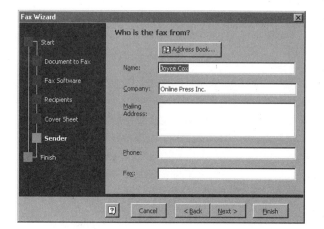

7. In the Name box, type *Al Pine* and press Tab. Then continue entering the information shown below, pressing Tab to move from box to box:

Company:	*In The Bag*
Mailing Address:	*1200 Yukon Ave.*
	Anchorage, AK 99502
Phone:	*907-555-1450*
Fax:	*907-555-1451*

8. Click Finish to display the fax header shown here (we've turned off the ruler so you can see more of the document):

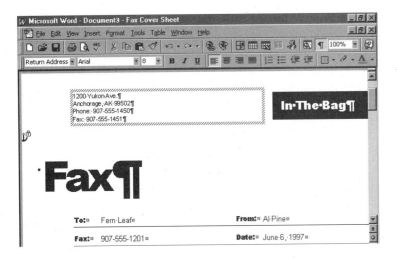

Complete the fax header by following these steps:

1. Replace the Phone placeholder with *907-555-1200* and the Pages placeholder with *1*.

2. Next, type *Glacier Series* over the Re placeholder, and delete the CC placeholder.

3. Double-click the box to the left of Please Reply. Word responds by putting a check mark in the box, like this:

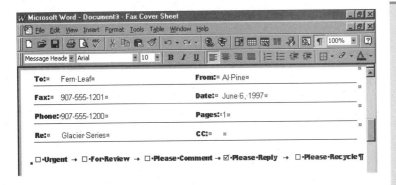

Now let's insert the text of the fax:

1. Delete •*Comments:* and the following space. Then select the [Click here and type any comments] placeholder.

What causes the check mark?

The row of check boxes at the bottom of the fax cover sheet header are actually form fields (see page 97) with a macro, or small program, attached to them. Double-clicking a check box runs the macro, which instructs Word to insert a check mark in the box. The topic of macros is beyond the scope of this book, but you can get more information by reading the discussions of macros in Word's online help.

2. Open Glacier Memo (the document you created in the last section), select the two main paragraphs, click the Copy button, and close the memo.

3. With the placeholder still selected, click the Paste button.

4. Save the fax with the name *6-06-97 Fax* (or the date of your fax) and then print and close it.

More Formatting Techniques

As you saw in the previous chapter, a well-designed document uses formatting to provide visual cues about its structure. In this section, we'll explore some more formatting techniques as we combine the FAQ from Chapter 2 and the memo from this chapter to make a flyer. Follow these steps:

1. Starting with a blank window, click the Open button on the Standard toolbar and double-click Frequently Asked Questions in the My Documents folder.

2. To safeguard the original FAQ file, choose Save As from the File menu and save the current version as *Flyer*.

Merging documents →

3. Press Ctrl+Home to be sure that the insertion point is at the top of the document, and choose File from the Insert menu to display this Insert File dialog box:

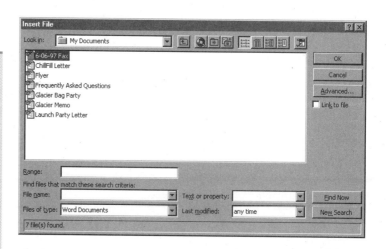

Painting formats

If you want to format a block of text with settings that you have already applied to another block of text, you can copy all the formatting in a simple three-step procedure. Select the text whose settings you want to copy, click the Format Painter button on the Standard toolbar, and then select the text you want to format. Word duplicates the formatting for the new selection.

4. Select Glacier Memo and click OK to merge its file into Flyer.

5. Press Ctrl+Home to move to the top of the combined document, and select and delete everything from the memo except the title and the two paragraphs (be sure to delete any blank paragraphs at the end of the memo).

6. Click the Save button on the toolbar to save the combined document, which should look like this:

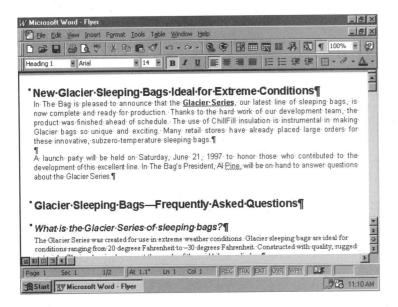

From now on, we won't tell you when to save the flyer, but you should do so at regular intervals to safeguard your work.

Making Titles Stand Out

As you know, we apply character formatting when we want to change the appearance of individual characters. Here we'll focus on the titles of the two "articles" in the new flyer. Let's get started:

1. Move to the top of the document, select the title of the memo, click the Center button on the Formatting toolbar to center the title, change the font to Times New Roman, and then change the size to 16 points.

Rebreaking titles and headings

As you create titles and headings for your Word documents, you may find that some of them would be more aesthetically pleasing if they broke to multiple lines or broke in a different spot. To rebreak a title or heading (or any other line of text), click an insertion point where you want the break to occur and press Shift+Enter. Word then inserts a line break, which it designates on the screen with a broken-arrow symbol.

2. Now select *Glacier Sleeping Bags—Frequently Asked Questions*, the title of the FAQ. Center the title, and change the font to Times New Roman and the size to 16 points.

3. With the title still selected, choose Font from the Format menu to display this dialog box:

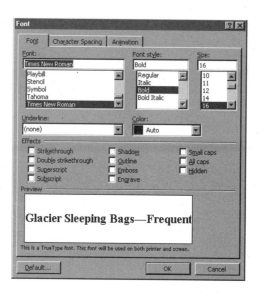

As you can see, the dialog box reflects the character formatting of the selected title. It also provides several options not available on the Formatting toolbar.

4. Click Small Caps in the Effects section to format the title in small capital letters with large initial capital letters, and then click OK.

If you want, you can experiment with some of the other options in the Font dialog box before moving on.

Adding Borders and Shading

To emphasize particular paragraphs, we can draw lines above and below or to the left and right of them, or we can surround the paragraphs with different styles of borders. Let's put a border around the FAQ title by following these steps:

AutoFormat

Word's AutoFormat feature analyzes all or part of a document and automatically assigns styles to its paragraphs based on how they are used and how they relate to other paragraphs. Word doesn't always reach the right conclusions after analyzing a document, but it usually gives you a good starting point for further formatting. To try this, choose Auto-Format from the Format menu. (To format only part of a document, select that part before this step.) You can then select the AutoFormat Now option to accept all the formatting or the AutoFormat And Review Each Change option to review and accept or reject each format in turn. You can use the Undo button to reverse the formatting if AutoFormat completely misses the mark.

1. With the title still selected, choose Borders And Shading from the Format menu to display the dialog box shown here:

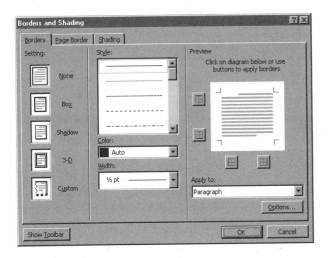

2. Click the arrow to the right of the Width box and select the 1½ pt single-line option.

Changing line styles

3. Click the Box setting. Word displays a preview on the right side of the dialog box.

4. Next click the Shading tab. In the Fill section, click Gray-25% (the third box in the second row) to fill the box around the title with a light gray color. Then click OK.

5. Click anywhere to remove the highlighting and see this:

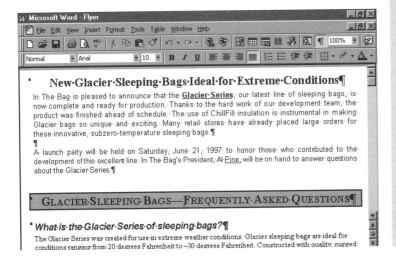

AutoFormat As You Type

By default, Word automatically formats certain elements of your documents, such as numbered lists. If you want to turn this feature off, choose AutoCorrect from the Tools menu and click the Auto-Format As You Type tab to view the settings available with this option. In the Apply As You Type section, deselect any of the features you want turned off. In the Replace As You Type section, you can specify whether Word should turn straight quotes (" ") to smart quotes (" "), use superscript with ordinals (1st), use fraction characters (½), change placeholder symbol characters and formatting, and create hyperlinks for Internet and network paths. In the Automatically As You Type section, you can control the treatment of lists and styles.

6. If you want, experiment with the other possible border and shading options.

Setting Up Multiple Columns

Newsletters and flyers often feature multicolumn layouts like those of magazines and newspapers. These layouts give us more flexibility when it comes to the placement of elements on the page, and they are often more visually interesting than single-column layouts. With Word, setting up multiple columns for an entire document couldn't be easier. We simply click the Columns button on the Standard toolbar and select the number of columns we want. And as you'll see if you follow these steps, when we want only part of a document to have a multicolumn layout, we select that part of the document before clicking the Columns button:

1. Select the text beginning with *What is the Glacier Series of sleeping bags?* to the period in the very last sentence of the *How do I order?* paragraph. (Don't select the paragraph mark.)

The Columns button

2. Click the Columns button. Word drops down this grid of columns:

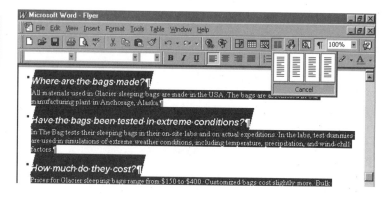

3. Point to the first column, move the mouse pointer across the three columns, and click. Word asks whether you want to switch to page layout view.

4. Click OK. Word reformats the text so that it snakes across the page in three columns. In normal view, Word puts a section break (a double dotted line with *Section Break (Continuous)* at its center) at the beginning of the selected text and another

at the end. However, because you are in page layout view, these section breaks are not displayed. The document now looks something like this:

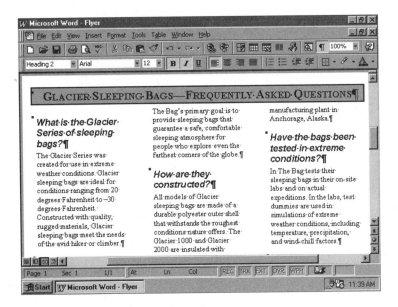

Creating Lists

The last paragraph of the FAQ contains three numbered items that would stand out better if they were set up as a list. Word has two built-in list formats: one for numbered lists and one for bulleted lists. Here's how to implement the numbered list format (the bulleted list format works the same way—see the tip on the next page for more information):

1. Use the scroll bar to move to the last paragraph, click an insertion point to the left of the number 1, and press Enter.

2. Click an insertion point to the left of the number 2 and press Enter. Word recognizes that consecutive paragraphs starting with numbers comprise a numbered list and responds by adding another 2 and a period in front of the new paragraph, giving both numbered paragraphs a hanging-indent format. This capability is called *AutoFormat As You Type* (see the tip on page 67).

3. Delete the extra 2, the period, and the space in the second numbered paragraph.

More column options

When you click the Columns button on the Standard toolbar and move the pointer across the grid to highlight the number of columns you want, you can select only up to four columns. However, if you hold down the left mouse button and drag to make your selection, you can select up to six columns. To format columns more precisely, choose Columns from the Format menu to display the Columns dialog box. Here, you can define the number of columns, the format, the width and spacing, and whether you want to display a dividing line between the columns. As you make your selections, Word displays a preview of the column formatting in the Preview box.

4. Repeat steps 2 and 3 for the number 3. Here are the results:

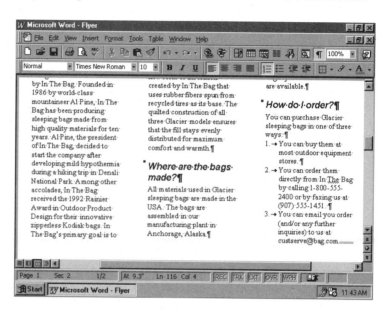

If you want to create a numbered list from scratch, type 1, a period, a space, and then the numbered item. When you press Enter, Word automatically formats the next paragraph as the next item of the numbered list. To return the next paragraph to regular formatting, click the Numbering button on the Formatting toolbar. (To turn off AutoFormat As You Type options altogether, see the tip on page 67.)

You can quickly convert existing text paragraphs to a numbered list by selecting the paragraphs and then clicking the Numbering button (see page 77).

Adding Headers and Footers

The flyer is currently only one page long. For documents that are longer than one page, we'll usually want to add a header or footer, so we'll show you how to do that next.

Headers are printed in the top margin of the page, and footers are printed in the bottom margin. With Word, we have many header and footer options. For example, we can create identical headers and footers for every page, a different header and footer for the first page, different headers and footers for left (even) pages and right (odd) pages, or different headers and footers for each section of a document.

Suppose we want a header to appear on all pages of the flyer except the first. For this demonstration, let's add more pages to the flyer, like this:

1. Press Ctrl+End to move to the end of the document, and then choose Break from the Insert menu to display this dialog box:

2. Accept the default Page Break option by clicking OK.

3. Now insert another page break using a different method: Press Ctrl+Enter. As you can see at the left end of the status bar, your document now has three pages.

4. Press Ctrl+Home to move to the top of the flyer.

Now let's tackle the header:

1. Choose Header And Footer from the View menu. Word dims the text of the document, outlines the space in which the header will appear with a dotted box, and displays the Header And Footer floating toolbar, as shown here:

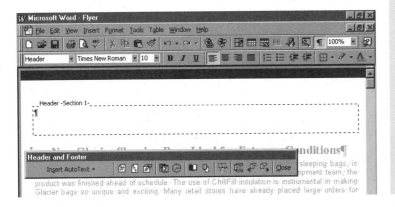

Adding footnotes

Footnotes are used to document sources and to give tangential tidbits of information when their inclusion in the main text would detract from the discussion. To add a footnote, simply click an insertion point after the word where you want the footnote reference mark to be placed. Then choose Footnote from the Insert menu to display the Footnote And Endnote dialog box. By default, Word automatically numbers footnotes and places them at the bottom of the page. (Click the Endnote option to have your reference appear at the end of the document.) To change the placement of footnotes or endnotes, the number format, or numbering options, click the Options button in the Footnote And Endnote dialog box and make the appropriate adjustments. When you click OK, Word inserts a superscripted 1 at the location of the insertion point and moves to the bottom of the page or the end of the document—depending on the option you have chosen—and waits for you to type the footnote/endnote text. (If you are in normal view, the footnote/endnote appears in a separate window with the Footnotes toolbar.) When you finish typing the text, click anywhere outside the footnote if you are in page layout view or click the Close button on the Footnotes toolbar if you are in normal view. To edit your footnotes, choose Footnotes from the View menu.

The Page Setup button

2. Click the Page Setup button on the Header And Footer toolbar to display the Layout tab of the Page Setup dialog box:

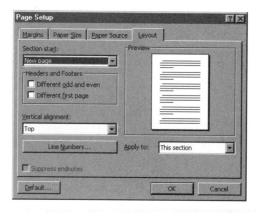

3. In the Headers And Footers section, select the Different First Page option and click OK. Word changes the header designation to read *First Page Header - Section 1*.

4. We're going to leave the first page header blank, so click the Show Next button on the Header And Footer toolbar to move to the next page, which begins section 3. (Section 2 is the three-column section on page 1.)

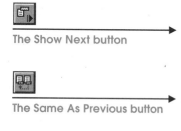

The Show Next button

5. Click the Same As Previous button to toggle it off, indicating that you want this header to be different from the first one.

The Same As Previous button

6. Now type *In The Bag*, press the Tab key twice, type *Page* and a space, and click the Insert Page Number button.

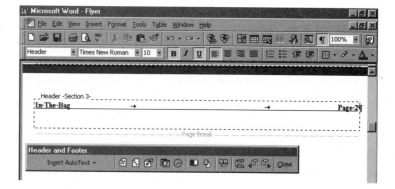

The Insert Page Number button

7. Select the entire header, click the Bold and Underline buttons, and press Home. The header looks like this:

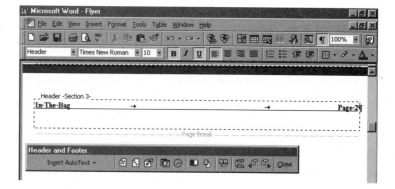

8. Click the Close button to return to page layout view.

Let's take a quick look at the flyer in print preview:

The Multiple Pages button

1. Click the Print Preview button. Then click the Multiple Pages button on the Print Preview toolbar to drop down a grid of "pages." Point to the left "page" in the top row, move the pointer over the center page, and click it. Word displays the first two pages of your document side by side, as shown here:

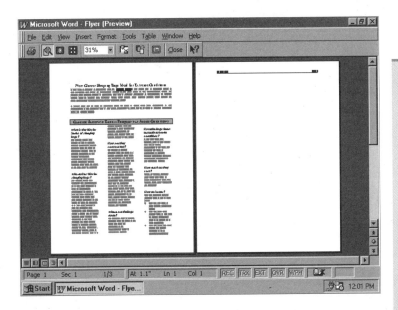

2. Press the Page Down key to see the third page, and then click the Close button on the Print Preview toolbar.

Formatting with Styles

We can work through a document applying formats to headings and other special paragraphs one by one, but Word provides an easier way: we can store custom combinations of formatting by defining the combination as a *style*. We can then apply that combination to a text selection or a paragraph simply by selecting the style from the Style drop-down list on the Formatting toolbar.

Every paragraph we write has a style. When we open a new blank document, it is based on the Blank Document template, and Word applies the Normal style to all paragraphs unless

More about page numbers

If you want your headers or footers to contain nothing but page numbers, you don't have to create a header or footer. You can have Word perform this chore for you. Choose Page Numbers from the Insert menu and in the Page Numbers dialog box, specify whether the numbers should appear at the top or bottom of the page, how they should be aligned, and if a number should appear on the first page. When you click OK, Word inserts page numbers in the document's header or footer. Whether you add page numbers this way or by clicking the Insert Page Number button on the Header And Footer toolbar, you can format them by clicking the Format button in the Page Numbers dialog box. You can select from five numbering schemes: Arabic numbers (1, 2, 3), lowercase/uppercase letters (a, b, c/A, B, C), and lowercase/uppercase Roman numerals (i, ii, iii/I, II, III). You can also specify whether chapter numbers should be included and select a starting number.

The Normal style →

instructed otherwise. The Normal style formats characters as 10-point regular Times New Roman and paragraphs as left-aligned and single-spaced. When we base a document on a template other than Blank Document, the styles included as part of that template become available, and as you saw earlier in this chapter, we can then create documents like the memo simply by filling in the paragraphs of the template.

Because we inserted the Glacier Memo file in Flyer, the memo's styles have been incorporated into the Flyer document. Check this out:

1. Click the arrow to the right of the Style box on the Formatting toolbar to drop down the Style list.

2. Scroll through the list. You'll see that Word has added the styles from the memo template, each displayed in its assigned formatting. Paragraph styles are preceded by a paragraph mark and character styles are preceded by an *a*.

3. Press the Esc key to close the list.

Using Word's Predefined Styles

As you learned in Chapter 2, Word comes with nine predefined heading styles, one for each of the heading levels we can designate when using the Outlining feature. Word also has predefined paragraph styles for a number of other common document elements, such as index entries, headers and footers, and footnotes. For a new document, Word lists only paragraph styles for Heading 1 through Heading 3, Normal, and the Default Paragraph Font character style. Word does not list the other predefined styles unless we insert one of those elements in the document. Then Word both applies the corresponding style to the element and adds the style name to the Style list.

When Word applies one of its built-in styles to an element, it uses the formatting that has been predefined for that element. Once the style is available on the Style list, we can apply it to other paragraphs. We can also redefine the style to suit the document we are creating, and we can create entirely new styles.

Character styles vs. paragraph styles

Character styles affect only the selected text, and these styles are applied on top of any paragraph formats assigned to the selected text. Paragraph styles affect the entire paragraph containing the insertion point. For example, you can apply a paragraph style that makes the font and size of an entire paragraph 12-point regular Arial, and then you can select the first word and apply a character style that makes just that word bold, italic, and underlined. Then you can apply a different paragraph style that makes the font and size of the entire paragraph 14-point regular Times New Roman, but the first word remains bold, italic, and underlined.

Creating Custom Styles

Although Word does a good job of anticipating the document elements for which we will need styles, we will often want to come up with styles of our own. For example, let's create a style for the first two paragraphs of the flyer. Suppose we want to delete the space between the paragraphs and indent their first lines so that it's easy to tell at a glance where one paragraph ends and the other begins. We'll also make the size of the characters slightly larger. Here's how to create a style with this combination of formatting:

1. Delete the paragraph mark between the first and second paragraphs.

2. Click an insertion point in the first text paragraph and choose Paragraph from the Format menu to display the dialog box shown here:

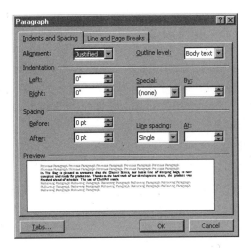

3. In the Indentation section, select First Line from the Special drop-down list. Word enters 0.5" in the By edit box as the default first-line indent and shows in the Preview box below how your text will look with this setting.

4. Change the setting in the By edit box to *0.15"*, and then change the After setting in the Spacing section to *6 pt*. Click OK.

5. Now select the entire paragraph and change the text to 12-point Times New Roman. Click anywhere in the paragraph below to remove the highlighting and see the results on the next page.

The Style dialog box

You can manage the available styles and create new ones by choosing Style from the Format menu. You can click the New button to define a new style, the Delete button to remove the selected style, and the Modify button to display a dialog box in which you can change the selected style. (See the tip on page 77 for another way to modify styles.) If styles occur in a particular sequence in a document, you can specify that one style should automatically follow another by selecting the first style, clicking the Modify button, and selecting a style from the Style For Following Paragraph drop-down list.

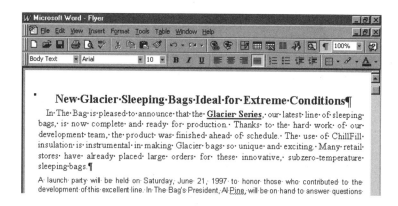

To assign a different name to the new style, follow these steps:

Naming a custom style

1. Click an insertion point in the first paragraph of the flyer and then click the Style box to highlight the style name in it.

2. Type *Indented Paragraph*, the name you want for this style, and press Enter. Word creates the style, adds its name to the Style list, and displays Indented Paragraph in the Style box to indicate that it is applied to the active paragraph.

3. Click an insertion point in the second paragraph of the flyer, drop down the Style list, and select the Indented Paragraph style. Word changes the style of the second paragraph so that its formatting is consistent with the first paragraph.

Now let's turn our attention to the FAQ part of the flyer. Suppose we want to justify these paragraphs and add a little space before each one. (Paragraphs with space before them are called *open paragraphs*.) Follow these steps:

1. Click an insertion point in the first text paragraph of the FAQ, right-click it, and choose Paragraph from the object menu.

2. Select Justified from the Alignment drop-down list in the top left corner of the Paragraph dialog box (the equivalent of clicking the Justify button on the Formatting toolbar).

3. In the Spacing section, change the Before setting to *3 pt* and click OK.

4. Now click the Style box to highlight the name in it, type *Open Paragraph* as this style's name, and press Enter.

Transferring styles to other documents

Once you have created a style for use in one document, you don't have to recreate it for use in others. You can simply copy the style to the new document. Or if you want the style to become a part of the set of styles available with a particular template, you can copy the style to that template. Simply choose Style from the Format menu, and in the Style dialog box, click the Organizer button. The Styles tab lists the styles available in the current document on the left. Open the desired template in the box on the right (you may have to click Remove File to clear the box first). Then select the style you want to copy from the box on the left and click the Copy button. Word copies the style to the designated template.

5. In turn, select each paragraph of the FAQ (including the numbered paragraphs) and then select Open Paragraph from the Style list to apply that style. (Some of the text wraps to the second page of the document. We'll fix that shortly.)

6. Select the second, third, and fourth paragraphs under the *How do I order?* heading and click the Numbering button on the Formatting toolbar to reapply the numbered-list format "on top of" the Open Paragraph style. The results are shown here:

The Numbering button

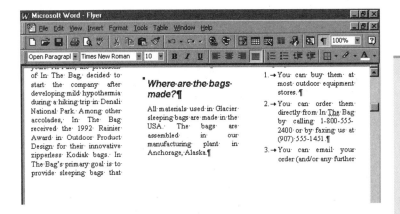

Hyphenating Documents

By default, Word does not hyphenate your text, but by hyphenating some words you can really improve the looks of the justified skinny columns of the FAQ part of the flyer. Follow these steps:

1. Press Ctrl+Home to move to the top of the document. (You may as well hyphenate all the text.)

2. Choose Language and then Hyphenation from the Tools menu to display this dialog box:

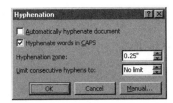

Modifying styles

To modify one of Word's default styles or one of your own, first select the text that uses the style you want to change and make the formatting changes. Then, to redefine the style to include the changes you have made, select it in the Style list. When Word displays the Modify Style dialog box, select the Update option to modify the existing style, or select the Reapply option to revert to the style's existing formatting. Click the Automatically Update check box if you want the style to be redefined whenever you make a change to text that uses it. (To turn off the Automatically Update option, choose Style from the Format menu, click Modify, deselect the Automatically Update check box, and click OK and then Close.) Click OK to implement your choices, or click Cancel to close the dialog box and leave your formatting changes intact without redefining the style. Once you redefine a style, all other occurrences of that style in your current document will be updated as well.

3. Select the Automatically Hyphenate Document option and click the Hyphenate Words In CAPS option to deselect it. Then click OK. Word quickly hyphenates the document.

4. Scroll through the flyer, noticing the effects of hyphenation. Many of the big spaces between words have disappeared, and the flyer now looks much more attractive.

Now let's fix the layout of the pages so that all of the text appears on the first page and the columns are more even:

1. Choose Page Setup from the File menu.

2. On the Margins tab, change the Bottom setting to 0.5", select Whole Document from the Apply To drop-down list, and then click OK.

3. Click an insertion point in front of the first word of the last line of the first column (*comfortable*, in our case), choose Break from the Insert menu, select Column Break, and then click OK. Word pushes the last line in the first column to the top of the second column.

4. Without moving the insertion point, press Enter to push the second column into better alignment with its neighbors.

5. Check the document in print preview to verify that all the text now fits on the first page. (If it doesn't, adjust the bottom margin and the position of the column break to make it fit.)

6. Close print preview, and then save and close the flyer.

With the features we have explored in the three chapters of Part One, you should have no trouble using Word to create useful documents for your work. In Part Two, we'll cover some of Word's more advanced features so that you can confidently create more complex word-processing documents.

BUILDING PROFICIENCY

In Part Two, we build on the techniques you learned in Part One to create even more sophisticated documents. After completing these chapters, you will be able to create most types of professional documents. In Chapter 4, you learn how to set up tabular lists and tables, and then you create a simple form. You also save a couple of documents as templates. In Chapter 5, we show you how to work with objects, including WordArt text, ready-made graphics, graphs, and spreadsheets. In Chapter 6, we wrap up the book with a discussion of mail merge, and you create both form letters and mailing labels.

Tables and Forms

First we show you how to use tabs to create simple tabular lists. Then we use Word's tables feature to create and format more complex tables. We also develop a letterhead using the tables feature. Finally, we create a simple form and show how to fill it in.

Dear Cliff:

Here is the information you requested:

Style	Weight	Base Price
Glacier 1000	3 lb. 9 oz.	$140.00
Glacier 2000	4 lb. 11 oz.	$225.50
Glacier 3000	5 lb. 9 oz.	$325.50

GLACIER SLEEPING BAGS GROSS SALES			
July-December 1997			
Month	Glacier 1000	Glacier 2000	Glacier 3000
July	$35,100.10	$45,500.45	$57,800.30
August	$32,450.40	$42,400.65	$52,000.00
September	$40,600.00	$61,250.30	$68,520.65
October	$52,700.65	$70,320.00	$89,630.85
November	$67,350.80	$89,850.50	$102,960.90
December	$102,000.90	$106,950.40	$119,320.75
TOTAL	$330,202.85		
AVERAGE	$55,033.81		

Call me if you have any questions.

Ida Down

IN THE BAG

Business
Travel
Expenses

Reason for Travel: Denver Show

Airfare:	$610.00	**Payment Method:**	Corporate C.C.
Meals:	$175.50	**Payment Method:**	Personal C.C.
Hotel:	$420.00	**Payment Method:**	Corporate C.C.

Miscellaneous (Cash):

Mileage:	$65.00
Parking:	$25.00
Tolls:	$0.00
Taxi:	$25.50
TOTAL:	$115.50

In the interests of clarity, we will want to display certain types of information in a table rather than in a narrative paragraph. In a table, individual items are easier to spot, and relationships between items are more obvious. With Word, we can use tabs to create simple tables, or we can design more complex and flexible tables using Word's tables feature. We cover both methods in this chapter, and we'll also teach you how to set up forms. Like tables, forms lend a structure to information, but their purpose is different. We use forms when we want to facilitate the input of information rather than display it.

Creating Tabular Lists

For simple tables, we can set tabs so that we can align information neatly in columns. This type of table is known as a *tabular list*. Follow these steps to create a tabular list now:

1. With Word loaded and a blank document on your screen, check that normal view is active and that the ruler is turned on. Then type the following:

   Dear Cliff: (press Enter twice)
   Here is the information you requested: (press Enter twice)

Setting tabs with the Tabs command

Instead of using the ruler, you can choose Tabs from the Format menu to display a dialog box in which you can set tabs. Enter the tab position in the Tab Stop Position edit box and click Set. Word adds the tab to the Tab Stop Position list below the edit box. You can specify how the text should be aligned at the tab and whether the tabs should have leaders. For example, if you create a table of contents for a report, you might want to set a Right tab with dot leaders to draw your readers' eyes from a heading across the page to a page number.

2. Type *Style* and press Tab. The insertion point jumps to a position on the screen that corresponds to that of the next tab setting, which is indicated by a tiny line on the gray bar below the ruler.

3. Type *Weight*, press Tab, type *Base Price*, and press Enter to end the first line of the list.

4. Choose Save As from the File menu, type *Sales Memo* as the filename, and then press Enter or click Save.

5. Now type the following, pressing Tab where indicated by the → and pressing Enter at the end of each line:

Glacier 1000	→	*3 lb. 9 oz.*	→	*$140.00*
Glacier 2000	→	*4 lb. 11 oz.*	→	*$225.50*
Glacier 3000	→	*5 lb. 9 oz.*	→	*$325.50*

We need to adjust the tab settings to align the sleeping-bag information with the headings, but first let's indent the entire list. (As a general rule, you should always apply all other formatting, including character formatting, to a list before setting tabs, because the slightest change can make the text columns jump annoyingly out of alignment.) Try this:

1. Select the four lines of the tabular list and click the Increase Indent button on the Formatting toolbar. Word indents the selected text to the first tab setting, as shown here:

The Increase Indent button

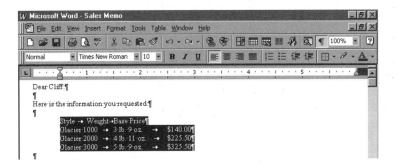

On the ruler, two triangular markers now sit on a small rectangular marker at the ½-inch mark. The top triangle controls how much the first line of the active paragraph is indented, and the bottom triangle controls how much the rest of the paragraph is indented. You can adjust the first-line or paragraph indent by manually dragging the corresponding triangle, or you can adjust both at once by dragging the rectangle, like this:

2. With the tabular list still selected, point to the rectangle at the ½-inch mark on the ruler, hold down the mouse button, and drag the rectangle to the left to the second tick mark (the ¼-inch mark). The two triangles move with the rectangle. When you release the mouse button, Word adjusts the indent for the entire list.

Adjusting indents with the ruler

Now let's align the columns. Notice that the weight descriptions push the dollar amounts so that they are not aligned with their column header. We need to set tabs so that the lines in the second column align at 1¼ inches and those in the third column align at 2½ inches. Follow these steps:

1. Without moving the selection, point to the 1¼-inch mark on the ruler and click the left mouse button once. A left-aligned

Default tab settings

By default, Word sets tabs every half inch across the page. You can adjust their position by choosing Tabs from the Format menu and changing the Default Tab Stops setting. When you set a custom tab, Word removes all the default tabs to the left of the new tab but retains the default tabs to the right.

The Tab button

tab marker (an *L*) appears on the ruler, and the items in the second column of all the selected lines jump to left-align themselves at that position on the screen.

2. Click the Tab button at the left end of the ruler. The icon on the button changes to indicate that clicking the ruler now will set a centered tab (an upside-down *T*), which would cause all the items in the column to center themselves on the tab's position.

3. Click the Tab button again to activate a right-aligned tab (a backwards *L*), and then click the ruler at the 2½-inch mark. The items in the third column of the selected lines jump to right-align themselves at that position. (Clicking the Tab button again would activate a decimal-aligned tab, which you can use to align numbers on their decimal points; see page 90.)

4. Press Ctrl+End to remove the highlight and move to the end of the memo, which now looks like the one shown here:

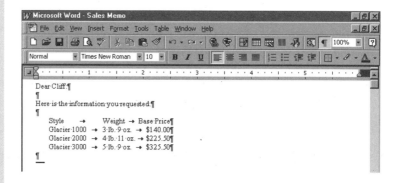

5. Press Enter once to add a blank line, and type *Call me if you have any questions*. Then press Enter four times and type *Ida Down*.

6. Save the memo. (Save frequently from now on.)

Creating Tables

As we said earlier, tables provide visual summaries of information and enable us to quickly grasp relationships that might be lost in narrative explanations. Creating tables in Word is a simple process. You specify the number of columns and rows

Other ways to create tables

You can create a table with specific column widths by choosing the Insert Table command from the Table menu and entering specifications in the Insert Table dialog box. From this dialog box, you can also move to the Table AutoFormat dialog box (see the tip on page 90). Yet another way to create a table is to use the Draw Table button on the Tables And Borders toolbar. Click the button to activate the drawing tool (the pointer turns into a pencil) and drag it diagonally to draw a box. When the box is the size you want for the table, release the mouse button. Next draw horizontal and vertical lines to create rows and columns. To remove a line, click the Eraser button on the Tables And Borders toolbar to activate the Eraser tool and drag over the line you want to erase. You can erase one border of a cell to merge cells either vertically or horizontally. To turn off either the Draw Table or Eraser tool, simply click the appropriate button to toggle it off. You can then edit and format the table just as you would any other table.

and then leave it to Word to figure out the initial settings. To demonstrate how easy the process is, we'll add a table to the memo we just created:

1. Click an insertion point to the left of the *C* in *Call* and then press Enter.

2. Press the Up Arrow key to move back to the empty paragraph you just inserted, and then click the Insert Table button to drop down a column/row grid.

The Insert Table button

3. Point to the top left square, hold down the left mouse button, and drag the pointer across four columns and down seven rows. The grid expands as you drag beyond its bottom edge, and Word shows the size of the selection below the grid. When you release the mouse button, Word inserts a table structure in the document like the one shown here:

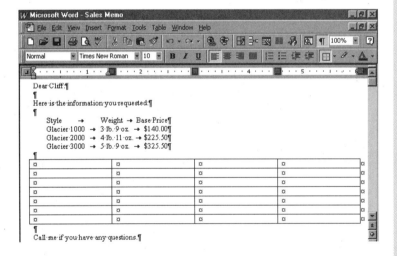

As you can see, Word has created a table with four equal columns, and the table automatically spans the width of the document's text column. The insertion point is in the first *cell* (the intersection of the first column and the first row). To make an entry in this cell, all we have to do is type, like this:

1. To enter column headings, type *Month* in the first cell and press Tab. The insertion point moves to the cell to the right.

Deleting/inserting rows and columns

To delete one or more rows or columns, select them and choose Delete Rows or Delete Columns from the Table menu. (If you don't select rows or columns first, the command is named Delete Cells, and choosing this command displays a dialog box in which you can specify what you want to delete.) To insert rows or columns, select the number of rows or columns you want to add, starting below the row or to the right of the column where you want them inserted. Then choose the Insert Rows or Insert Columns command or use the Insert Rows or Insert Columns button on the Standard toolbar (see page 89). To delete the entire table, select it and choose Delete Rows. If you press the Delete key to accomplish any of these tasks, the contents of the cells are deleted but not the cells themselves.

2. Type *Glacier 3000* and press Tab to move the insertion point to the next cell. Type *Glacier 2000* and press Tab. Finally, type *Glacier 1000* and press Tab. Here are the results so far:

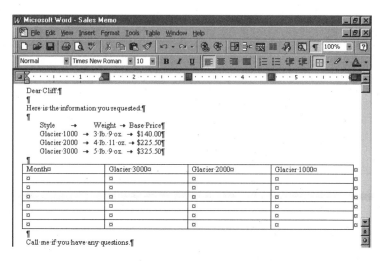

Notice that pressing Tab at the end of the first row moved the insertion point to the first cell in the second row.

3. Finish the table by typing the entries shown below, pressing Tab to move from cell to cell. (Pressing Shift+Tab moves the insertion point to the previous cell, and you can also use the Arrow keys and the mouse to move around.)

July	*$57,800.30*	*$45,500.45*	*$35,100.10*
August	*$52,000.00*	*$42,400.65*	*$32,450.40*
September	*$68,520.65*	*$61,250.30*	*$40,600.00*
October	*$89,630.85*	*$70,320.00*	*$52,700.65*
November	*$102,960.90*	*$89,850.50*	*$67,350.80*
December	*$119,320.75*	*$106,950.40*	*$102,000.90*

Looking over the table, we can see one or two changes that would make it more effective. We discuss ways to edit tables in the next section.

Rearranging Tables

We can rearrange the rows and columns in a table in much the same way that we rearrange text. Let's switch the Glacier 3000 column with the Glacier 1000 column:

Moving around a table

Printing headings for multi-page tables

If you create a table that is longer than one page, you can instruct Word to print the table headings at the top of all the pages on which the table appears. Simply select the row(s) containing the headings and choose Headings from the Table menu. (You can't see the headings in normal view.) To turn off the printing of table headings on multiple pages, click an insertion point anywhere in the original heading row(s) and choose Headings from the Table menu to toggle it off.

1. Click any cell in the Glacier 1000 column and choose Select Column from the Table menu. (You can choose Select Row to select the row containing the active cell, or Select Table to select the entire table.)

Selecting a column

2. Point to the selected column, hold down the mouse button, drag the shadow insertion point to the beginning of the Glacier 3000 heading, and release the mouse button. The Glacier 1000 column moves to the left of the Glacier 3000 column.

Moving a column

3. Now select the Glacier 2000 column and move it to the left of the Glacier 3000 column. The results are shown here:

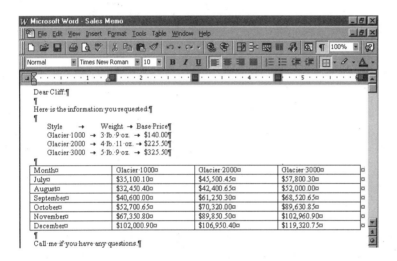

Changing Column Width

We can adjust column widths in three ways: by moving the column markers designated with grids on the ruler, by dragging column borders, or by using the Cell Height And Width command. Follow these steps to change the widths of the columns in the example table:

1. With the insertion point located anywhere in the table, move the pointer over the left end of the ruler, below the Tab button. When the pointer changes to a two-headed arrow with a ToolTip that reads *Move Table Column*, hold down the left mouse button and drag to the right until the text in the first column of the table is aligned with the text in the first column of the tabular list above. (This can be tricky. If the table jumps

Resizing rows

In page layout view, you can manually adjust the size of table rows. Simply move the pointer over the row's bottom border and drag up or down to the desired size. If you hold down the the Alt key as you drag, Word displays the exact row height in the adjacent vertical ruler. (You can also drag the gray bars in the vertical ruler to adjust row height.)

too far, click the Undo button and try again.) The first column's marker has moved about ¼ inch to the right on the ruler.

Changing column widths
with the ruler

2. Next point to the column marker on the ruler between the first and second columns and drag the marker to the left until the column is just wide enough for its entries. Then drag the column marker between the second and third columns to adjust the width of the second column to hold its entries.

3. Now adjust the third and fourth columns using a different method. First point to the right border of any cell in the third column, and then drag the two-headed pointer to the left to about the 2¾-inch mark on the ruler. Repeat this procedure for the fourth column so that the right edge of the table ends at the 3¾-inch mark. Here are the results:

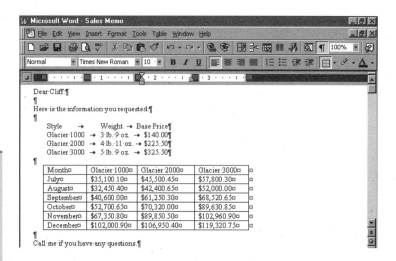

Word wrapping in tables

If text in your table wraps to more than one line, it is because Word's default row-height setting is Auto. As a result, Word wraps long entries to the number of lines needed to display the entries in their entirety, adjusting the height of the row as necessary. If you want all entries to appear on only one line, select the table, choose Cell Height And Width from the Table menu, select Exactly from the Height Of Rows drop-down list, specify an At setting that is a couple of points larger than the font size used in the table (for example, 12 pt if the font size is 10), and click OK.

Adding a Title

Suppose we want to add a row above the table to contain a title. The first step is to insert a new row:

1. Move the pointer into the invisible selection bar adjacent to the first row of the table, and click to select the entire row. Or click any of the cells in the top row and choose Select Row from the Table menu.

2. Click the Insert Rows button on the Standard toolbar. Word inserts the number of rows you have selected—in this case, one.

The Insert Rows button

Next, we need to join the cells of the new row to create one large cell to accommodate the table's title. Joining cells is a simple procedure, as you'll see if you follow these steps:

1. Click the Tables And Borders button to display the Tables And Borders toolbar. If Word says you must switch to page layout view, click OK. (If necessary, double-click the tool-bar's title bar to dock it below the Formatting toolbar.)

The Tables And Borders button

2. With the first row of the table selected, click the Merge Cells button on the Tables And Borders toolbar. Word combines the cells into one large cell that spans the table.

The Merge Cells button

3. Now enter the title. Click an insertion point in the top row, type *GLACIER SLEEPING BAGS GROSS SALES*, press Enter, and type *July-December 1997*. Here are the results:

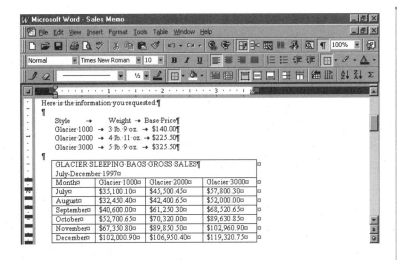

Formatting Tables

Having made all the necessary structural changes to the table, let's add some finishing touches. First, we'll format the title and headings:

1. Select the first two rows of the table, click the Center button, and then press Home to remove the highlighting and view the results.

Sorting tables

You can use the Sort Ascending and Sort Descending buttons on the Tables And Borders toolbar to sort the information in a table. First, select the column containing the information you want to sort by—you might sort a table of contribution information by company name. Then click the Sort Ascending button to sort starting with A (or the lowest digit), or click the Sort Descending button to sort starting with Z (or the highest digit). For more complex sorts, click an insertion point anywhere in the table and choose Sort from the Table menu. In the Sort dialog box, you can designate up to three columns to sort by—you might sort the contribution information by company name, then by Zip code, and then by contribution amount.

2. To make the table title and the headings in the *Month* column bold, point to the left of the word *GLACIER* in the title, hold down the mouse button, and drag downward through the first column. Then click the Bold button.

Well, that was simple. Now let's see how to decimal-align the numbers in the second, third, and fourth columns. This involves setting decimal tabs in each of these columns. Follow these steps:

Setting a decimal tab

1. Click the Tab button at the left end of the ruler until it is set to a decimal tab (an upside-down *T* with a period).

2. To align the numbers in the Glacier 1000 column on the decimal point, drag through the six cells containing numbers in that column to select them, and then click the 1³/₈-inch mark on the ruler (see the graphic below) to set a decimal tab where you want the decimal points to line up.

3. Repeat the previous step to decimal-align the Glacier 2000 and Glacier 3000 numbers in about the middle of their columns. The table now looks like this:

Table autoformats

An easy way to apply formatting to a table is by using Word's table autoformats. Simply click an insertion point inside the table you want to format and click the Table AutoFormat button at the right end of the Tables And Borders toolbar, or choose Table AutoFormat from the Table menu. In the Table AutoFormat dialog box, you can choose from a variety of table styles. Click a name in the Formats list, and Word will display a sample of the format in the Preview box. You can then modify the style using the options in the lower portion of the dialog box. Click OK to complete the changes and you instantly have a great-looking table.

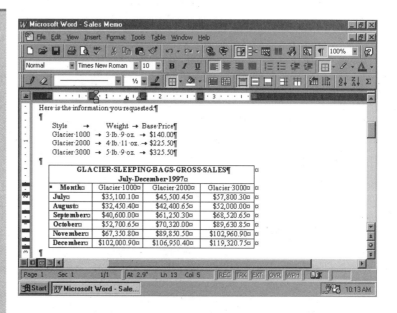

By default, Word puts a ½-pt single line gridline around each cell and a ½-pt single line border around the whole table.

Before we wrap up this section, let's experiment with grid-lines and table borders:

1. With the insertion point anywhere in the table, choose Select Table from the Table menu.

2. Click the arrow to the right of the Line Weight box on the Tables And Borders toolbar and select ¾ pt from the drop-down list.

3. To change the line weight of the gridlines only, click the arrow to the right of the Border button on the Tables And Borders toolbar to display a palette of options.

The Border button

4. Click Inside Border (the second option in the bottom row) to change all the gridlines to ¾ pt.

5. Now click the arrow to the right of the Line Style box and select the double line style (the eighth option in the list).

6. Change the line weight to 1½ pt, click the arrow next to the Border button, and click Outside Border to create a 1½-pt double-line border. Here are the results:

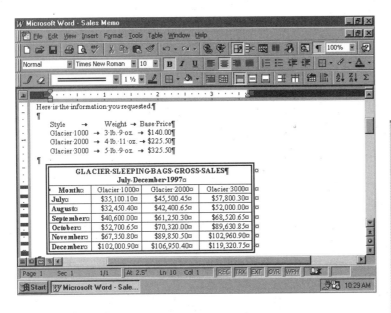

Turning off gridlines

By default, Word gives tables a border and gridlines. If you want a table without a border or grid-lines, select the table, click the Border button from the Tables And Borders toolbar, and then click No Border. To display grid-lines that won't print but help you manipulate the structure of the ta-ble, choose Show Gridlines from the Table menu. Choose Hide Gridlines to turn them back off.

7. Save your work.

Calculations in Tables

In Chapter 5, we demonstrate how to import a spreadsheet into Word (see page 133), but Word 97 includes a variety of spreadsheet functions that we can use to build formulas directly in Word tables. Let's add a totals row to the gross sales table and see how easily we can turn a Word table into a spreadsheet. Here are the steps:

Adding a row for totals

1. Start by adding a row to the bottom of the table. Click an insertion point to the right of the entry in the table's last cell (just before the end-of-cell marker) and press Tab.

2. In the first column of the new row, type *TOTAL* and then press Tab to move to the next column.

The AutoSum button

3. Click the AutoSum button on the Tables And Borders toolbar. Word quickly looks above the selected cell and calculates the sum of the values entered in the cells above.

4. Press Tab to move to the next column.

5. Click the AutoSum button again to total the current column of values.

6. Repeat step 5 for the final column. The table now looks like this one:

Totaling cells to the left

If your table is structured so that the values you want to total are oriented from left to right instead of top to bottom, you can click the AutoSum button for the first row you want to total. For the remaining rows, however, choose Formula from the Table menu, change the =SUM(ABOVE) formula in the Formula edit box to =SUM(LEFT), and click OK.

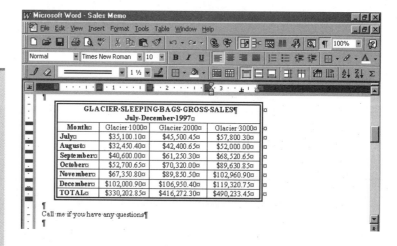

With the first release of Word 97, when you used the Auto-Sum button to total a column of values and the column heading contained a number, that number was included in the total. (The =SUM(ABOVE) formula also behaved this way.) Double-check the math the first time you use AutoSum. If your result is wrong because of a number in a heading, such as Glacier 1000 in our example, use the Formula command on the Table menu and follow steps 2 through 5 in the next section, using the SUM functions and precise cell specifications to total the values.

CAUTION!

Let's see how to average the gross sales:

1. Add a row to the bottom of the table, type *AVERAGE* in the first column of the new row (you may have to adjust the width of the column), and press Tab.

2. Choose Formula from the Table menu to display the dialog box shown here:

Using the AVERAGE function

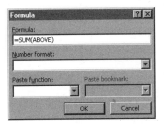

3. Select the contents of the Formula edit box, and press Delete to erase the default entry.

4. Type an = sign, and then click the down arrow to the right of the Paste Function edit box to display a list of functions. Click AVERAGE. Word pastes the function and a set of parentheses in the Formula edit box.

5. The numbers you want to average are in the second column—column B—and in rows 3 through 8 of the table, so type *B3:B8* between the parentheses, and click OK.

Updating calculations

After you add a formula to a Word table, you may need to update the calculation if you change the data or if you add/delete a row. To update the calculation, select the calculation field and press the F9 key. If your table contains a formula that references specific cells, such as the Average formula in our example, you must open the Formula dialog box and adjust the cell references manually to update the calculation.

6. Repeat steps 2 through 5 for the other two columns, using C3:C8 and D3:D8 as the cell specifications.

7. Save the memo, print it, and then close the document.

You might want to take some time to explore Word's functions on your own. They may not let you create sophisticated stock projections or loan analyses, but if your spreadsheet formulas usually involve nothing more complex than a few mathematical calculations, being able to create spreadsheets within Word may save you considerable time.

When Is a Table Not a Table?

Sometimes we can use Word's tables feature to create elements of a document not normally thought of as "tables." For example, tables can be used to create a letterhead or fax cover sheet form. By using the table structure, we can more easily manipulate blocks of text that appear side by side, because they are contained in different cells of the table.

In this section, we'll create a simple header for a business travel expense form. Follow these steps to see how easy it would be to use this technique to create a letterhead using Word's tables feature:

Turning a table into text and vice versa

To convert a table to tabular text, select the entire table and choose Convert Table To Text from the Table menu. Indicate how you want Word to separate the information that's now in columns and click OK. Word removes the table grid and separates the text that was in columns as you indicated. To turn a block of regular text separated by tabs into a table, select all the tabular text and click the Insert Table button on the toolbar. If the text is separated by characters other than tabs, select the text, choose Convert Text To Table from the Table menu, indicate the number of columns and how the information is separated, and then click OK.

1. Click the New button to open a new document on your screen.

2. Click the Insert Table button and then drag across two columns and one row.

3. In the table's first cell, type *IN THE BAG*. Press Tab and type *Business Travel Expenses*.

4. Save the document as *Travel Expenses Form*.

The header doesn't look like much yet, so let's add some formatting to jazz it up a bit. Follow these steps:

1. Click to the left of the text in the first cell to select it, and then change the font to bold, 48-point Arial.

2. Let's make the text white and the background black. First click the arrow to the right of the Shading Color button on the Tables And Borders toolbar to display a color palette.

The Shading Color button

3. Click Black (the first option in the top row). Word changes the background to black, although you cannot see this effect because your text is still selected.

4. Without moving the selection, choose Font from the Format menu. Click the arrow to the right of the Color edit box and select White.

Changing font color

5. Next click the Small Caps check box in the Effects section.

6. Now click the Character Spacing tab and click the arrow to the right of the Spacing edit box. Select Expanded and in the By edit box, change the setting to 7.5 pt. (This formatting change will increase the amount of space between each character in the selected text.) Click OK to confirm your changes and then click anywhere in the document. Your header should look something like this:

Changing character spacing

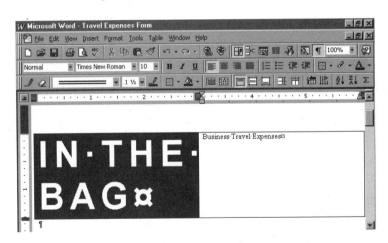

7. So that the text stays on one line, increase the width of the first column to about the 5-inch mark.

Now let's quickly format the second column of the header:

1. Select the second cell and change the font to 14-point Times New Roman.

2. Use the Cell Height And Width command in the Table menu to change the width of the column to *1"*. Because of the cell width, the text wraps to three lines.

The Center Vertically button

3. To shift the text lower in the cell so that it aligns better visually with the first cell, click the Center Vertically button on the Tables And Borders toolbar. Press Ctrl+Home to see the results shown here:

4. Turn off the Tables And Borders toolbar by clicking the Tables And Borders button.

5. Save the document, which we'll use in the next section when we create a form.

Creating Forms

So far, we have used tabular lists and tables to display certain types of information in an organized manner. We could create invoices, purchase orders, or similar documents using these techniques, but there's an easier way. By creating a special type of Word document called a *form*, we can simulate printed forms in such a way that we can press the Tab key to skip over the text entries that don't change, which are called *labels*, and jump to the sections that need to be filled in, which are called *form fields*. (Although we didn't point it out at the time, we showed you how to fill in a form in Chapter 3 when we created a memo based on a Word template. We also filled in a form when we used the Fax Wizard to create a fax cover sheet. Both of those documents used a form for their header information.)

Form fields

To see how to create forms, let's design a business travel expenses form for In The Bag. Follow these steps to set up the form using the document now on your screen:

1. With Travel Expenses Form open, press Ctrl+End and then press Enter a couple of times to add some space between the header and the form you are about to create.

2. Right-click either the Standard or Formatting toolbar and choose Forms from the object menu to display the Forms toolbar.

Displaying the Forms toolbar

3. If necessary, dock the Forms toolbar below the Formatting toolbar.

Here's how to create form fields using the toolbar buttons:

1. Type *Reason for Travel:* and press Tab.

2. Click the Text Form Field button. Word inserts the field at the insertion point, as shown here:

The Text Form Field button

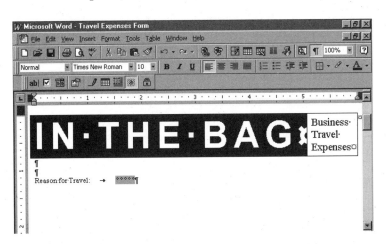

3. Press Enter to start a new line, type *Airfare:*, and press Tab.

The Form Field Options button

4. Click the Text Form Field button and then click the Form Field Options button to display this dialog box:

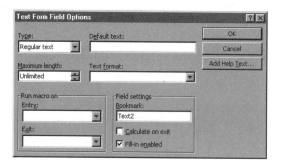

5. Click the arrow to the right of the Type box and select Number. Next click the arrow to the right of the Number Format edit box and select the fifth option (the one that contains dollar signs). Then click OK.

The Drop-Down Form Field button

6. Click an insertion point after the Airfare form field, press Tab, type *Payment Method:*, press Tab again, and click the Drop-Down Form Field button on the Forms toolbar.

7. Click the Form Field Options button, type *Corporate C.C.* in the Drop-Down Item box, and click the Add button. Then type *Personal C.C.* in the Drop-Down Item box, click the Add button, and click OK. Word inserts the first item in the list as the default—in this case, *Corporate C.C.*

8. Click an insertion point after the new field and press Enter to add a blank line. Then move the pointer into the selection bar to the left of the Airfare line and, when the pointer changes to a hollow, right-pointing arrow, click to select the line.

9. Click the Copy button to copy the line, press Ctrl+End to move the insertion point to the blank line at the bottom of the document, and click the Paste button twice.

10. Change the second Airfare to Meals and the third one to Hotel. Your form now looks like the one shown on the facing page.

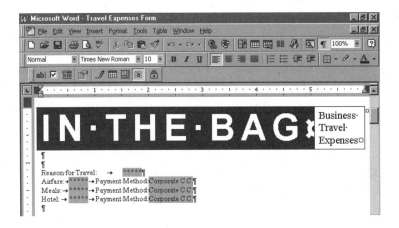

Editing Forms

The travel expenses form is starting to take shape. If we want to edit the form's labels, we can use ordinary text editing techniques, but if we want to edit the form's fields, we have to use the Form Field Options dialog box. To demonstrate, let's edit some of the fields to include help text that will appear in the status bar when the fields are selected:

1. Click the Reason for Travel form field once to select it, and then click the Form Field Options button on the Forms toolbar.

2. In the Text Form Field Options dialog box, click the Add Help Text button to display this dialog box:

Adding help text

3. Click the Type Your Own option and type *Enter the name of the show or conference* in the box below. Then click OK

Check box form fields

To add a check box field to a form, click the Check Box Form Field button on the Forms toolbar. You can then click the Form Field Options button to change settings such as the size of the check box or the default value (whether it is checked on or off by default).

twice. (You won't see the help text displayed in the status bar until you turn on document protection, which we'll do on page 105.)

4. Now right-click the Airfare field and choose Properties from the object menu to display the Text Form Field Options dialog box again.

5. Click the Add Help Text button, click the Type Your Own option, and type *Enter the total dollar amount* in the box below. Click OK twice.

6. Repeat steps 4 and 5 to add the same help text to the Meals and Hotel fields.

Now let's edit the drop-down list fields by adding some help text. Follow these steps:

1. Double-click the first Payment Method field to automatically open the Drop-Down Form Field Options dialog box.

2. Click the Add Help Text button, click the Type Your Own option, and type *Click the down arrow to display the payment method options.* Click OK twice to enter the changes.

3. Repeat steps 1 and 2 to add the same help text to the other two Payment Method fields.

4. When you have finished adding the help text, click the Save button to save your work.

Formatting Forms

Now that we have the fields set up the way we want them, we can format the form to spruce up its appearance, as well as make it easier to read. We want to make some adjustments to the tabs, but before we do that, we should take care of any other character and paragraph formatting. To format the text of a form, we use the same techniques we use in any other type of Word document. Let's apply some basic formatting right now:

Using AutoText for help

To speed up the entry of often-used help text, you can create AutoText entries (see page 34). You can then click AutoText Entry in the Form Field Help Text dialog box and select the appropriate AutoText name from a list to have the corresponding text appear in the status bar.

1. Select the entire form (except the header) and change the font size to 12.

2. Next select the *Reason for Travel:* label (but not the field that follows it) and click the Bold button. Repeat this step for all of the other labels.

3. Now select the entire form again (except the header) and choose Paragraph from the Format menu.

4. In the Spacing section, change the Before and After settings to 3 pt and click OK. Your form should now look like this:

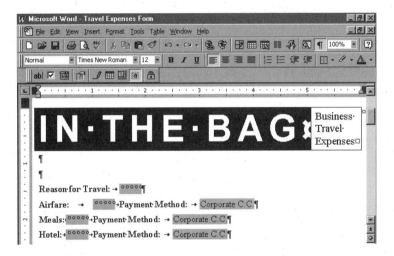

As you can see, the tab settings need to be adjusted so that the fields line up. Let's make those adjustments now:

1. With the form selected, click the Tab button until it displays a left-aligned tab (see page 84), and then click the 1½-inch mark on the ruler. Word inserts a left-aligned tab on the ruler and moves the text appropriately.

2. Click the 2¾-inch mark on the ruler to set another tab, and then set a final tab at the 4¼-inch mark.

   Hmmm... The space between the fields is a little too wide. But instead of starting over, let's adjust the tabs on the ruler, as follows:

1. With the form still selected, point to the tab at the 2¾-inch mark on the ruler, hold down the left mouse button, and drag

More about using the ruler to set tabs

When you manually set a tab using the ruler (or using the Tabs command), the tab takes effect for the paragraph that contains the insertion point or selected paragraphs only. To remove a custom tab, point to it, hold down the left mouse button, and then drag the tab away from the ruler. Double-clicking a tab on the ruler opens the Tabs dialog box, where you can quickly customize that tab. For example, you can change its Alignment or Leader settings. (See the tip on page 82 for more information about the Tabs dialog box.)

the tab to the left to the 2¼-inch mark. Word adjusts the position of the *Payment Method* label.

2. Now repeat step 1 to move the tab at the 4¼-inch mark to the 3¾-inch mark on the ruler. The form now looks like this:

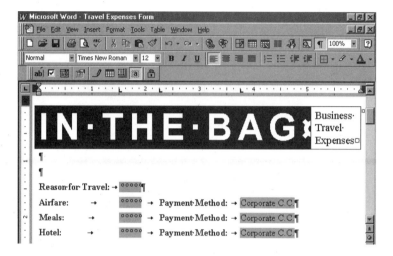

Calculations in Forms

Forms like the travel expenses form often involve calculations. Why perform them manually when we can have Word do them for us? As you saw earlier on page 93, if we enter the values to be calculated in a table, Word can use cell references to perform the calculations. Let's experiment by adding a table of miscellaneous cash expenses that need to be totaled, by following these steps:

1. Press Ctrl+End to move to the bottom of the Travel Expenses Form document. Press Enter a couple of times to add some space between the upper portion of the form and the table you are about to add.

2. Type *Miscellaneous (Cash):* and then press Enter.

3. Click the Insert Table button, hold down the mouse button, and drag through two columns and five rows in the table grid.

4. In the first cell, type *Mileage:*, press Tab, and click the Text Form Field button on the Forms toolbar.

5. Click the Form Field Options button and change the Type to Number and the Number Format to the fifth option (the one with the dollar signs). Then click OK.

6. Click an insertion point in the first cell of the second row and type *Parking:*. Press the Down Arrow key and type *Tolls:*. Press the Down Arrow key again and type *Taxi:*.

7. Next copy the form field in the Mileage row and paste it into the second column of the Parking, Tolls, and Taxi rows. Your table should look like this one:

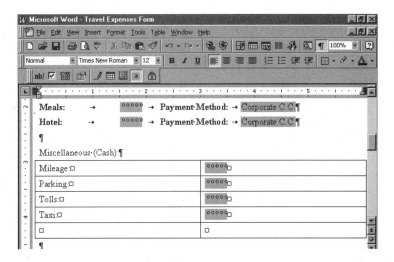

Now it's time to add the formula that will total the miscellaneous cash expenses. Follow these steps:

1. Click an insertion point in the first cell of the last row. Type *TOTAL:* and press Tab.

Inserting a calculation field

2. Click the Text Form Field button on the Forms toolbar and then click the Form Field Options button.

3. In the Type drop-down list, select Calculation.

4. Click an insertion point in the Expression edit box after the equal sign (=) and type *SUM(B1:B4)*. This expression tells Word to total the values in the first through fourth cells of the second column (B).

5. In the Number Format drop-down list, select the fifth option and then click OK.

Let's finish up the form with some simple formatting:

1. Select the title above the table and click the Bold button.

2. Select the first column of the table and make it bold.

3. Move the pointer to the column border between the two columns and drag to the left to about the 1½-inch mark so that the form fields in the table left-align with the form fields in the top section of the form. The form should now look something like this one:

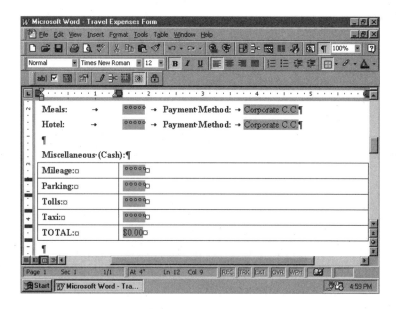

4. Save the form.

Saving Forms as Templates

Once we create a form, we will usually want to save it as a template. We can then access it at any time and fill in the appropriate information, just as we did in Chapter 3 with the memo template (see page 57). But before we can save our form as a template, we must *protect* the document so that only the fields can be changed. Let's protect the Travel Expenses Form document now:

1. Click the Protect Form button on the Forms toolbar.

The Protect Form button

2. Now try to click an insertion point in the header or labels, or in front of an empty paragraph mark. You can no longer change text in the document unless it appears in a form field.

Now let's save the document as a template so that we can try filling it in:

1. First close the Forms toolbar by right-clicking it and deselecting Forms on the object menu.

2. Next choose Save As from the File menu. In the Save As Type drop-down list, select Document Template. Word changes the Save In location to the Templates subfolder of the Program Files/Microsoft Office folder on your hard drive.

3. Double-click the Other Documents folder and click Save to save the Travel Expenses Form template in that folder.

4. Close the template.

Filling in Forms

We now have a travel expenses form template available for use at any time, but we have yet to see how the form works. Let's open the template now and fill in some information for a trade show in Denver. Follow these steps:

1. Choose New from the File menu, and on the Other Documents tab, double-click the Travel Expenses Form icon. Word opens the form with the Reason for Travel form field highlighted.

2. First save the document by choosing Save As from the File menu, typing *Denver Show Expenses* as the filename, and clicking Save.

More about document protection

Word offers several types of document protection via the Protect Document command on the Tools menu. In addition to protecting all but the fields of a form, you can select the Forms option and then click the Sections button to protect sections of the form only. Or, to protect a document from changes by other people but allow them to annotate (add comments to) the document, select the Comments option. You can allow changes to the document but tell Word to keep track of the editing by selecting the Tracked Changes option. And you can assign a password of up to 15 characters that must be entered before Word will unprotect a document. (Passwords are case-sensitive.)

3. Type *Denver Show* in the Reason for Travel field and press Tab. Word skips over the Airfare label and moves to its field.

4. Type *610* and press Tab. Word automatically formats the number as currency, as you specified earlier when you created the form field.

5. A corporate credit card was used for the plane tickets, so press Tab to leave the entry as is.

6. In the Meals field, type *175.5*. Press Tab, click the down arrow to the right of Corporate C.C., and select Personal C.C. from the drop-down list. Then press Tab.

7. Type *420* in the Hotel field, press Tab twice to leave the payment method as is, and then type the following numbers in the appropriate form fields, pressing Tab to move from one field to the next:

Mileage: *65*
Parking: *25*
Tolls: *0*
Taxi: *25.5*

8. Press Tab again. Word moves to the top of the document, skipping the calculation field.

9. Scroll down to the TOTAL field, which contains *$0.00*.

Does this mean that Word has not completed the calculation? Not at all. Word simply has not been told to update the contents of the TOTAL field. We could attach a macro to this field to prompt updating. However, we can accomplish the same thing by making a simple adjustment in the Options dialog box and printing the form, so let's take this easier route:

1. Choose Options from the Tools menu and click the Print tab.

2. In the Printing Options section, click the Update Fields check box to turn it on, and then click OK.

Saving form data only

If you want to accumulate the data items entered in multiple copies of a form in a database, you can save only the data by choosing Options from the Tools menu, clicking the Save tab, and selecting the Save Data Only For Forms option. Then choose Save Copy As from the File menu to have Word create a text-only file with each data item enclosed in quotation marks and separated from adjacent items by commas. This file is then ready to be imported into a database.

3. Print the form by clicking the Print button. After you have printed the form, the number in the calculated field is displayed on your screen. Look at page 81 for a sample of what the printed form looks like.

4. Save and close Denver Show Expenses.

Customizing Form Templates

We've now seen how to create and fill in a Word form, but what if we want to create another form that is similar to an existing one? Simple. As a demonstration, let's quickly customize the business travel expenses form to create a form that tracks marketing project expenses:

1. Choose New from the File menu, and on the Other Documents tab, double-click Travel Expenses Form.

Basing a new template on an existing one

2. Choose Save As from the File menu and change the Save As Type setting to Document Template.

3. When Word moves to the Templates subfolder of the Program Files/Microsoft Office folder, double-click the Other Documents folder, type *Marketing Project Expenses Form* as the filename, and click Save.

Now let's customize the form:

1. Display the Forms toolbar by right-clicking a toolbar and choosing Forms from the object menu.

2. Click the Protect Form button to turn off form protection so that you can customize the header and labels for the new form.

Turning off form protection

3. Select the words *Business Travel* in the form header and replace it with *Marketing Project*. (Adjust the column width if necessary.)

4. Next change *Reason for Travel* to *Project* and then continue changing the labels as shown on the next page.

Airfare	*Radio*
Meals	*Printing*
Hotel	*Magazine*
Miscellaneous (Cash)	*Miscellaneous Expenses*
Mileage	*Freight*
Parking	*Office Supplies*
Tolls	*Design Costs*

5. Change all *Payment Method* labels to *Payment Terms*.

6. Select the Taxi row in the table and choose Delete Rows from the Table menu. The form now looks like this:

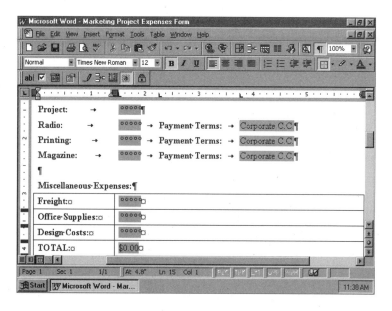

Now let's adjust some of the form fields:

Editing a calculation field

1. Because you have deleted a row in the table, double-click the TOTAL form field, change the cell reference in the Expression edit box from B4 to B3, and click OK.

2. Double-click the first Payment Terms form field, and with Corporate C.C. selected in the Items list, click Remove. Click Remove again to delete Personal C.C. from the list.

3. In the Drop-Down Item edit box, type *Net 30*, click Add, type *Net 60*, click Add, type *Net 90*, click Add, and then click OK.

4. Select the next Payment Terms form field and delete it. Then copy and paste the first Payment Terms form field to the next Payment Terms field.

5. Repeat step 4 to update the last Payment Terms form field.

6. Finally, double-click the Project form field, click the Add Help Text button and change *show or conference* to *project* and then click OK twice.

7. Click the Protect Form button and close the Forms toolbar. Your form now looks something like the one shown below. (We've switched to normal view, reduced the magnification, and turned off the ruler to display more of the form.)

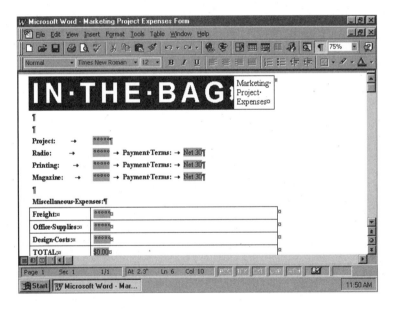

8. Save and close the template.

9. If you want, open a new document based on the Marketing Project Expenses Form template and try filling in the form.

As you have seen, tables and forms give us two ways to display information that we create in Word. In the next chapter, we'll look at ways we can use information created in other programs in our Word documents.

Graphics, Graphs, and Spreadsheets

We demonstrate how to use text to dress up documents using WordArt by creating a letterhead template and a masthead template. Then we import and manipulate a graphic. We create a graph with Microsoft Graph, and finally we import a spreadsheet from Excel as a table.

In The Bag is pleased to announce that the **Glacier Series**, our latest line of sleeping bags, is now complete and ready for production. Thanks to the hard work of our development team, the product was finished ahead of schedule. The use of ChillFill insulation is instrumental in making Glacier bags so unique and exciting. Many retail stores have already placed large orders for these innovative, subzero-temperature sleeping bags.

In The Bag is pleased to announce that the **Glacier Series**, our latest line of sleeping bags, is now complete and ready for production. Thanks to the hard work of our development team, the product was finished ahead of schedule. The use of ChillFill insulation is instrumental in making Glacier bags so unique and exciting. Many retail stores have already placed large orders for these innovative, subzero-temperature sleeping bags.

In The Bag is pleased to announce that the **Glacier Series**, our latest line of sleeping bags, is now complete and ready for production. Thanks to the hard work of our development team, the product was finished ahead of schedule. The use of ChillFill insulation is instrumental in making Glacier bags so unique and exciting. Many retail stores have already placed large orders for these innovative, subzero-temperature sleeping bags.

In The Bag is pleased to announce that the **Glacier Series**, our latest line of sleeping bags, is now complete and ready for production. Thanks to the hard work of our development team, the product was finished ahead of schedule. The use of ChillFill insulation is instrumental in making Glacier bags so unique and exciting. Many retail stores have already placed large orders for these innovative, subzero-temperature sleeping bags.

Dear Cliff:

Here is the information you requested:

Style	Weight	Base Price
Glacier 1000	3 lb. 9 oz.	$140.00
Glacier 2000	4 lb. 11 oz.	$225.50
Glacier 3000	5 lb. 9 oz.	$325.50

GLACIER SLEEPING BAGS GROSS SALES July-December 1997			
Month	Glacier 1000	Glacier 2000	Glacier 3000
July	$35,100.10	$45,500.45	$57,800.30
August	$32,450.40	$42,400.65	$52,000.00
September	$40,600.00	$61,250.30	$68,520.65
October	$52,700.65	$70,320.00	$89,630.85
November	$67,350.80	$89,850.50	$102,960.90
December	$102,000.90	$106,950.40	$119,320.75
TOTAL	$330,202.85	$416,272.30	$490,233.45
AVERAGE	$55,033.81	$69,378.72	$81,705.58

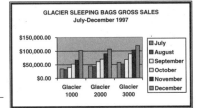

GLACIER SLEEPING BAGS GROSS SALES
July-December 1997

1997 GLACIER INCOME			
	3rd Quarter	4th Quarter	Total
Sales	$435,622.85	$801,085.75	$1,236,708.60
Selling Expenses	$130,686.86	$240,325.73	$371,012.58
Marketing Expenses	$43,562.29	$80,108.58	$123,670.86
Overhead	$87,124.57	$160,217.15	$247,341.72
Total Expenses	$261,373.71	$480,651.45	$742,025.16
Net Income	$174,249.14	$320,434.30	$494,683.44

While following the examples in the preceding chapters, you've learned a lot about Word's formatting capabilities and how to combine formats to create professional-looking documents. However, there may be times when the needs of a particular document exceed Word's capabilities. That's when we will want to enlist the help of other programs.

In this chapter, we start by demonstrating how to create special effects with text and how easily we can incorporate graphics into Word documents. Then we create graphs to visually present facts and figures. And for those times when you've already set up your information in a spreadsheet or database program and don't relish the thought of having to recreate it in Word, we'll show you how to import a spreadsheet or database as a Word table.

Text as Graphics

We have seen in earlier chapters some ways to format text to make it more visually appealing. But sometimes, this type of text formatting won't be quite spectacular enough. Here we'll look at a couple of techniques for giving documents more pizzazz. You can then experiment on your own with different ways of combining effects to create the look you want.

Creating Special Effects with WordArt

Want to create a text wave across the page or rotate a title to grab people's attention? That's the specialty of the Insert WordArt button on the Drawing toolbar. (In previous versions of Word, WordArt was a separate program, but now this capability is part of Word.) By embedding WordArt objects in our documents, we can produce an eye-catching look that can be handled by almost any printer.

Creating a Letterhead Template

For our first example, let's experiment with WordArt by quickly creating a letterhead for In The Bag. Follow the steps on the facing page.

Objects

An object is an element that originated outside the document where it now exists. It can be a block of text, a graphic, a table, a graph, and so on. You can incorporate objects into your documents in three ways: 1. You can copy and paste an object into a document, in which case the copy becomes an integral part of the document and is stored with it. 2. You can embed the object in the document, in which case it is stored with the document but retains information about the program that created it. If you want to change the object, double-click it to open it in the source program, edit the object, and close the program to return to the document with the changes in place. 3. You can link the object to the document, in which case the object exists in a separate file but is displayed in the document. Any changes you make to the object's file will be reflected in the version displayed in the document. (See the tip on page 134 for more information about embedding and linking.)

1. With a new, blank document on your screen, click the Drawing button on the Standard toolbar to display the Drawing toolbar along the bottom of your screen. (If you are not in page layout view, Word switches to it now.)

The Drawing button

2. Press Enter and then press the Up Arrow key to move back to the top of the page.

The Insert WordArt button

3. Next click the Insert WordArt button on the Drawing toolbar to display this WordArt Gallery dialog box:

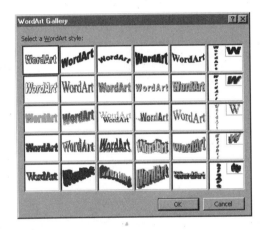

4. Click the second option in the fourth row and click OK to display this dialog box:

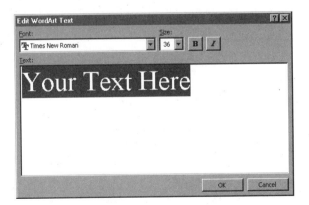

5. Type *IN THE BAG* and click OK to embed the object in the shape we chose and display the WordArt toolbar, as shown on the next page.

The WordArt object is "floating" at the top of the document. Let's resize it to make its shape more triangular:

1. Either dock the WordArt toolbar or close it. (Read the adjacent tip if you want to explore some of its features.)

2. With the WordArt object selected, as indicated by the presence of white squares called *handles*, point to the middle handle on the right side. When the pointer turns into a two-headed arrow, drag inward about an inch.

3. Next drag the bottom middle handle downward about half an inch. The WordArt object now looks something like this:

More WordArt options

The WordArt toolbar comes with a variety of buttons. To edit the WordArt text or change its font and font size, click the Edit Text button. To change the style, click the WordArt Gallery button to redisplay its dialog box. To change the color, size, or position, or the way regular text wraps around the WordArt object, simply click the Format WordArt button. The remaining buttons allow you to alter the shape, rotation, letter height, orientation, alignment, and character spacing of the WordArt object. You can also change the shape of the object by dragging the yellow diamond that appears to its left up or down. As you drag it, the dotted outline shows the approximate shape the object will assume when you release the mouse button.

Not bad for a start. To finish off the letterhead, let's reposition it and add an address below the company name. Here we go:

1. To reposition the WordArt object so that it appears centered at the top of the page, move the pointer over the WordArt text. When it turns into a four-headed arrow, drag the object so that its base sits at about the 1¼-inch mark on the vertical ruler and its peak sits at about the 3-inch mark on the horizontal ruler.

   Repositioning a WordArt object

2. Press Ctrl+End and press Enter until the insertion point is about a ¼ inch below the WordArt object. Then click the Center button on the Formatting toolbar.

3. Type *1200 Yukon Avenue, Anchorage, AK 99502*. Then press Enter again to add a blank line.

4. Select the address text, change the font size to 11, and then make it bold.

5. Fine-tune the placement of the WordArt object so that it is centered above the address. Here are the results:

Because In The Bag is likely to use this letterhead often, it makes sense to save the letterhead document as a template. Follow the steps on the next page.

Floating vs. inline objects

By default, Word inserts Word-Art objects as "floating" objects that are inserted on a separate drawing layer so that you can position them exactly where you want them. Also by default, the objects are anchored to the paragraph that contained the insertion point when you created them, and the objects will move with that paragraph. To control how an object interacts with the text of your document, click the Format WordArt button on the WordArt toolbar, click the Wrapping tab of the Format WordArt dialog box, and specify a wrapping style. For example, you can specify that the text should wrap around, through, or above and below an object. On the Position tab, you can deselect the Move Object With Text option to break the object's link with its paragraph mark.

1. Choose Save As from the File menu.

2. In the Save As dialog box, select Document Template from the Save As Type drop-down list, select an appropriate folder within the Templates folder (Letters & Faxes is a good choice), type *Letterhead* in the File Name box, and click the Save button. Then close the new template.

Creating a Masthead Template

Now let's do something a little more complex. This time, we'll use WordArt and the Drawing toolbar to design a masthead template for In The Bag with the company's masthead down the left side of the document and space for text, such as a press release, to the right. Follow these steps:

1. Click the New button on the Standard toolbar to open a new document.

2. So that we can put the masthead to the left and the text to the right, we need to set up columns in the document. Click the Columns button and drag through two columns.

3. Next choose Break from the Insert menu, select Column Break, and click OK to move the insertion point to the top of the second column.

4. Click the Insert WordArt button on the Drawing toolbar, select the last option in the top row, and click OK.

5. Type *IN THE BAG*, change the text size to 80, and make it bold. Click OK to return to your document, where the Word-Art object appears to float in the middle of the page.

Let's move the WordArt object into the desired location:

1. Move the pointer over the WordArt object, and when the pointer changes to a four-headed arrow, drag the object to the left side of the page and then downward about an inch from the top of the page, as shown here:

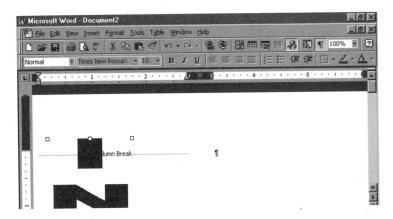

2. Scroll the bottom of the page into view and then drag the bottom middle handle of the WordArt object downward. Release the mouse button when you have about a 1 inch bottom margin.

3. Click the Print Preview button to see these results:

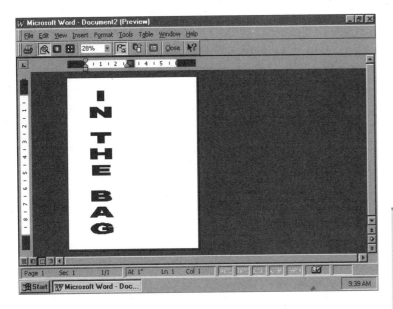

4. Click the Close button to return to page layout view, make any other necessary adjustments, and then save the document as a template called *Masthead*. (Save often from now on.)

Let's add a side border to the object to visually separate the masthead from the text of the press release, which we will add later. Follow the steps on the next page.

Editing WordArt objects

If you want to make changes to a WordArt object after you have inserted it in a document, double-click the object to display the Edit WordArt Text dialog box as well as the WordArt toolbar. You can then edit the text or use different toolbar buttons to make adjustments. When you're finished, click anywhere outside the WordArt frame to return to your document.

The Line button

The Line Style button

1. Deselect the WordArt object by clicking anywhere in the document. Then click the Line button on the Drawing toolbar.

2. Point about a ¼ inch to the right and a ½ inch below the bottom of the WordArt text, hold down the left mouse button, and drag upward to about a ½ inch above the WordArt text. (If the line is crooked, simply move the mouse to the left or right until the line straightens up.) Then release the mouse button.

3. With the line selected, click the Line Style button on the Drawing toolbar and select the 1½ pt line style from the list of options. The masthead template now looks like the one shown here in print preview:

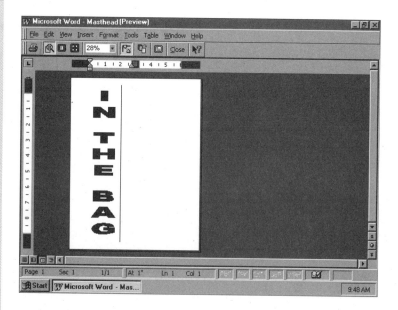

Adding page borders

With Word 97, you can add a border around each page of your document. To add a page border, choose Borders And Shading from the Format menu and then click the Page Border tab. Select the options you want and click OK. You can select from more than 160 border art styles in the Art drop-down list to apply a fancy border instead of a line border. If you want the border to appear only on a particular side of the page, click Custom in the Setting section. Then in the Preview section, click where you want the border to appear. To make the border appear only on a particular page or section of the document, click the appropriate option in the Apply To drop-down list. If you need to specify the exact location of a page border, you can click the Options button and then make your specifications. To delete a page border, redisplay the Page Border tab of the Borders And Shading dialog box and click None in the Setting section.

4. If you need to lengthen or shorten the line, point to its top or bottom handle and drag in the appropriate direction.

Now let's add some dummy press-release text to the template. (When we want to create a new press release based on this template, we can simply replace this text.) Follow these steps:

1. First adjust the size of the masthead column. Point to the column marker on the ruler, and when the pointer changes to a double-headed arrow, drag the marker to the left until the dotted vertical line aligns with the side border you just drew.

INVOICE

Tel.: 01343 813273
Fax.: 01343 813171

No. 5908

MORGANS

VIDEO :: TELEVISION :: ELECTRICAL

61 CLIFTON ROAD · LOSSIEMOUTH

M.. 17|4| 19 98

....

VAT Reg. No. 604 8068 48

UFESA JUG   19-95

PAID
CASH

SUB TOTAL	
VAT @	
TOTAL £	19-95

VAT included
unless shown separately

W/w 94
Page 121

2. Click an insertion point in the second column and open Glacier Memo (the document you created in Chapter 3).

Copying text using a scrap

3. Click the Restore button (the middle button) at the right end of Word's title bar so that part of the Windows 95 desktop is displayed.

4. Select the first text paragraph of the memo (the one that follows the heading) and drag it onto the desktop. When a plus sign appears below the pointer, release the mouse button. Word creates a document "scrap" icon on the desktop, representing your copied text, as shown here:

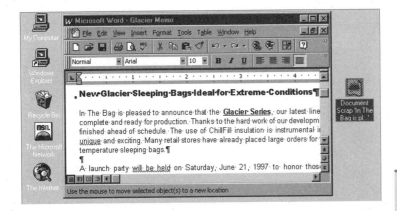

5. Close Glacier Memo and then drag the document scrap icon in front of the paragraph mark in the second column of the masthead template. Word inserts the text like this:

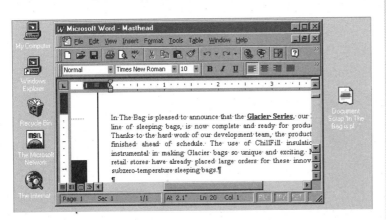

Document shortcuts

In addition to being another handy way to copy text from one document to another, a scrap is useful as a sort of bookmark. After spending several hours editing and formatting a long document, you can select the text you have worked on most recently in the document. Hold down the *right* mouse button, and drag the selection to the Windows 95 desktop. Then choose Create Document Shortcut Here from the object menu that appears. The next time you want to work on the document, simply double-click the shortcut icon to start Word with your document open and the selected text still highlighted, ready for you to pick up your work where you left off.

6. Maximize the Word window again and then select the newly inserted paragraph (including the paragraph mark that follows it) and click the Copy button.

7. Press Enter to insert an extra paragraph mark after the text paragraph and then click the Paste button.

8. Repeat step 7 twice more so that you have a total of four paragraphs, as shown here (we've reduced the magnification to 25% to show all the paragraphs):

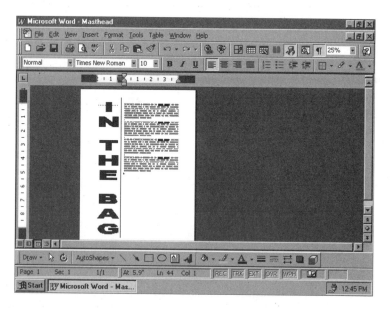

9. Save the template but don't close it. Then turn off the Drawing toolbar.

Adding a Drop Cap

A simple way to add a designer touch to a document is to use Word's built-in *drop cap* (for *dropped capital letter*) format. Drop caps are used in the first paragraph of each chapter in this book. Drop caps can also enhance newsletters, reports, and other documents that receive public scrutiny. Let's insert a drop cap in the first paragraph of the press release text:

1. Click an insertion point to the left of the first paragraph and press Enter to add some space above it.

Inserting special symbols

Sometimes you may want to use special symbols in a document, such as a pointing hand to draw the reader's attention. To insert a special symbol, position the insertion point, choose Symbol from the Insert menu, and select the font (Wingdings is a good one if you're looking for cute little pictures). Then click the symbol you want, click Insert, and click Close. If you use a symbol often, you can create a keyboard shortcut for the symbol by clicking the Shortcut Key button in the Symbol dialog box and specifying a shortcut that starts with the Ctrl or Alt key or a combination of the two.

2. Choose Drop Cap from the Format menu to see this dialog box:

By default, Word makes the first letter of the active paragraph the height of three lines of text. You can adjust the drop cap's font, height, and distance from the following text in the above dialog box.

3. Select the Dropped option and click OK. Then click anywhere in the first paragraph, which now looks like this:

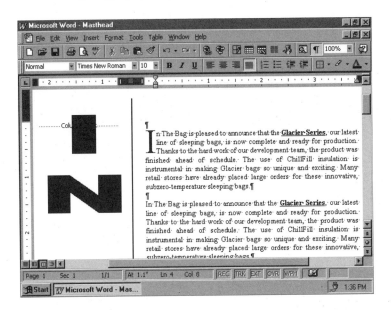

Importing Graphics

Word 97 comes with a collection of ready-made graphics files suitable for many different types of documents. We'll use one

Ready-made graphics

of these files and the press release we've been working on to demonstrate how easy it is to import graphics into Word documents.

When Word was installed on your computer, not all of the available graphics files were copied to your hard disk. Several other files can be viewed and imported into a document from Word's installation CD-ROM. In our examples, we use a couple of these graphics. If you do not have Word's installation CD-ROM, substitute any of the graphics that are available to you.

As a demonstration, we'll place the same graphic at the top and bottom of the press release. Follow these steps:

1. Click an insertion point to the left of the blank paragraph mark at the top of the press release text, press Enter once to add a bit more space, and then press the Up Arrow key once.

Inserting a graphic →

2. If it's available, insert Word's installation CD-ROM, and choose Picture and then Clip Art from the Insert menu to display the dialog box shown below. (If Word reminds you that more clip art is available on the installation disk and you don't have the disk at hand, click OK.)

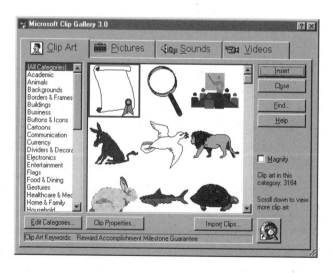

Supported graphics formats

You can insert graphics created with a program other than Word directly or by using a graphics filter. You don't need to use a graphics filter for EMF, JPG, PNG, BMP, RLE, DIB, or WMF graphics. You do need a graphics filter for DXF, CGM, CDR, EPS, GIF, PCD, PCT, DRW, PCX, TIF, TGA, and WPG graphics. If the graphics filters were not installed with Word, you can run Word's setup program to install them at any time.

3. Click the Borders & Frames category on the left side of the dialog box, scroll the previews on the right side, and select the mountain scene.

4. Click Insert to add the graphic at the top of the template and display the Picture toolbar as shown here:

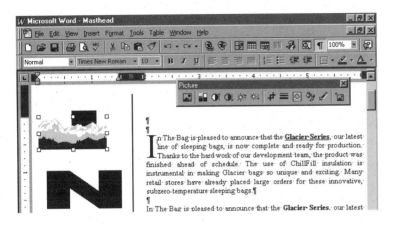

Sizing and Positioning Graphics

After we import a graphic, we can change its size and shape to suit the needs of our document. For example, we might want to turn the graphic into a small logo, or we might want to enlarge it so that it occupies most of the page. Let's experiment a bit:

1. Double-click the title bar of the Picture toolbar to dock it at the bottom of the screen.

2. If necessary, select the graphic by clicking it. A frame with handles appears around the graphic.

3. To increase the graphic's size, point to the handle in the bottom right corner, and when the pointer changes to a two-headed arrow, drag it downward and to the right.

If we drag the corner handles, we change the size of the graphic without changing the ratio of its width to its height. If we drag the handles in the middle of the sides of the frame, we do change this ratio. We can control the width-to-height ratio more precisely by changing settings in a dialog box instead of dragging. Follow the steps on the next page.

Drawing your own graphics

You can create your own simple drawings in Word by using the tools on the Drawing toolbar. Click the Drawing button on the Standard toolbar to switch to page layout view and to display the Drawing toolbar across the bottom of your screen. Use the Line, Arrow, Rectangle, and Oval buttons to draw those shapes. You can also click the AutoShapes button to display a pop-up menu of options that allow you to create a variety of more complex shapes. Then use the remaining buttons to manipulate your drawing in a variety of ways—for example, you can change its color and orientation.

The Format Picture button

1. With the graphic selected, click the Format Picture button on the Picture toolbar. When Word displays the Format Picture dialog box, click the Size tab to see these options:

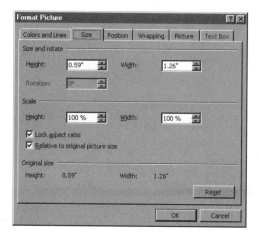

Floating vs. inline graphics

As with WordArt objects, graphics are floating by default (see the tip on page 115). You can convert a floating graphic to an inline graphic (one that is not on a separate drawing layer but is inserted directly in the document at the insertion point) by selecting the graphic, clicking the Format Picture button on the Picture toolbar, clicking the Position tab, and deselecting the Float Over Text check box. However, you then lose some formatting flexibility. For example, the options on the Wrapping tab, which enable you to control how text wraps around the graphic, are no longer available. When your graphic is floating, you can also wrap text by clicking the Text Wrapping button on the Picture toolbar and selecting an option from the pop-up menu.

2. In the Scale section, deselect Lock Aspect Ratio. Then set the Height option to 100% and the Width option to 50%, and click OK. Here's the result:

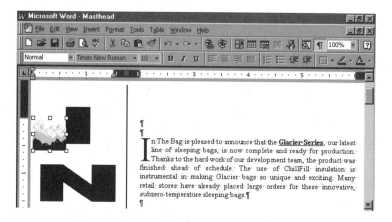

If we want to use only part of the graphic, we can change the size of the frame that contains it without changing the size of the graphic itself. This adjustment has the effect of "cropping" away the parts of the graphic that we don't want to be visible. Here are the steps:

1. With the graphic selected, click the Format Picture button on the Picture toolbar.

2. On the Picture tab of the Format Picture dialog box, change the Bottom setting in the Crop From section to 0.2" and click OK. When the dialog box closes, this is what you see:

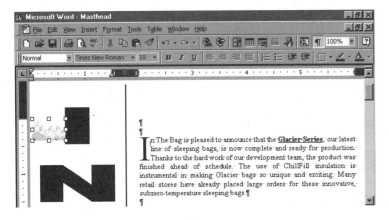

When you are working with graphics in Word documents (not templates), you can use the Crop button on the Picture toolbar to crop graphics. Select the graphic, click the Crop button, use the cropping tool to drag the appropriate handle to change the size of the graphic's frame, and then click the Crop button again to turn off the cropping tool.

The Crop button

3. Click the Reset Picture button on the Picture toolbar to restore the original graphic in its unscaled and uncropped size and proportions.

The Reset Picture button

After all that experimenting, let's be more precise about the graphic's size and location:

1. Click the Format Picture button on the Picture toolbar and on the Size tab, set the Height to *1* and the Width to *4*. Then click the Position tab and set the Horizontal setting to *2* and the Vertical setting to *0*.

2. Click OK to return to the document.

Depending on the width of the masthead column and the graphic you selected, you may have to adjust the settings to position the graphic exactly where you want it.

Editing graphics

To change a graphic you have created or one you have added using the Picture command, click the graphic to display the Picture toolbar. You can then use the buttons on the Picture toolbar to achieve the desired effect. When you are finished, click anywhere outside the graphic to return to your document with the updated graphic in place.

Copying Graphics

For fun, let's put the same graphic at the bottom of the press release text with this simple copy-and-paste procedure:

1. With the graphic selected, click the Copy button and then click the Paste button.

2. Click the arrow to the right of the Zoom box and change the magnification to 25%.

3. Drag the new copy of the graphic below the press release text. Here are the results:

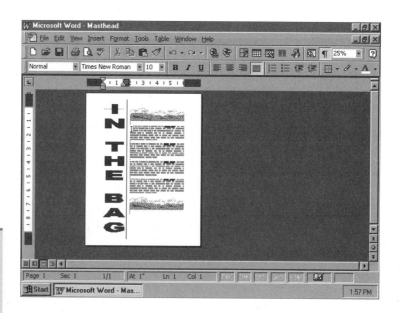

Using Graphics as Watermarks

Now let's add another graphic to the template to serve as a *watermark*. A watermark is a logo, picture, or text that appears "behind" a document. (Diplomas and stock certificates often sport watermarks.) To add a watermark to the masthead template, we can insert it in a header or footer so that the watermark will appear on every page of the document. Follow these steps:

1. Return the document magnification to 100% and choose Header And Footer from the View menu.

2. Click the Show/Hide Document Text button on the Header And Footer toolbar. Word hides all of the text and graphics in the press release.

The Show/Hide Document Text button

3. Choose Picture and then Clip Art from the Insert menu to display the dialog box shown earlier on page 122.

4. Select a clip art image and then click Insert. (We chose the camping scene from the Sports & Leisure category.) Your screen now looks something like this:

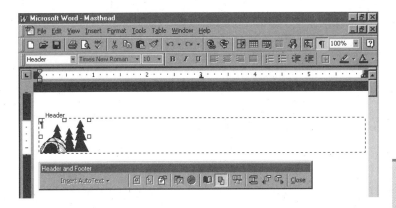

5. Next click the Format Picture button on the Picture toolbar.

6. On the Picture tab, click the arrow next to the Color edit box in the Image Control section and select Watermark.

7. Display the Wrapping tab and click None.

8. On the Size tab, change the Height setting in the Size And Rotate section to *2.5*"and the Width setting to *4*".

9. On the Position tab, type *2* as the Horizontal setting, type *3* as the Vertical setting, and click OK. Word positions the watermark in the desired location and adjusts the brightness and contrast of the graphic as appropriate for a watermark.

10. Choose Header And Footer from the View menu to return to the template and then click the Print Preview button to view the results, shown on the next page.

Using text boxes

For more flexibility with text, you can insert a text box into a document and then type the text directly into the box. Word treats text boxes as objects that can be positioned and sized on the page just like any other object. To try this, either choose Text Box from the Insert menu or click the Text Box button on the Drawing toolbar. Then drag a box in the document using the cross-hair pointer. When you release the mouse button, Word displays a text box with the insertion point located inside it, waiting for you to type your text. Once you type the text, you can format and edit it in the usual way. You can also use buttons on the Drawing toolbar to format the text box or choose Text Box from the Format menu to adjust its size, position, and text wrapping settings.

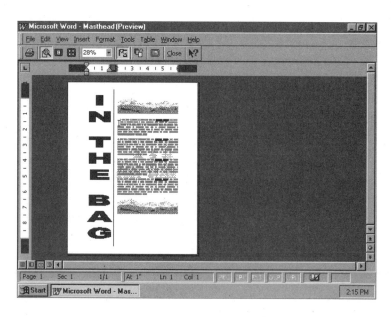

If you need to make any further adjustments to the watermark, return to the Header And Footer view, click the Show/Hide Document Text button, and click the watermark graphic to select it. Then either manually move or resize it, or click the Format Picture button and make your changes in the dialog box.

11. When everything is as you want it, save the masthead template and close it. If necessary, close the Picture toolbar.

We've thrown a lot of graphics into this example. For your own documents, you'll want to limit the use of graphics to avoid a cluttered look that makes your message hard to read.

Using Graph

With Word, we can cut or copy charts and graphs from other applications and then paste them into a Word document. But Word also comes with Microsoft Graph, a program we can use to create graph objects based on information in a Word document. Let's experiment using part of the table we constructed in the memo in Chapter 4. Follow these steps:

1. Open the Sales Memo document and save it as *Sales Memo 2*.

2. In normal view with Zoom at 100%, click an insertion point below the table, and press Enter twice to add some space.

Turning off graphics display

Inserting graphics in a document can slow down the rate at which you can scroll through the text. With inline graphics (see the tip on page 124), you can increase the scrolling speed by choosing Options from the Tools menu, clicking the View tab, clicking Picture Placeholders in the Show section, and then clicking OK. Word substitutes placeholders (empty frames) for the graphics. Reverse this procedure to turn on graphics display.

3. Select rows two through eight of the table—everything but the title, total, and average rows—and click the Copy button.

4. Choose Object from the Insert menu to display this dialog box:

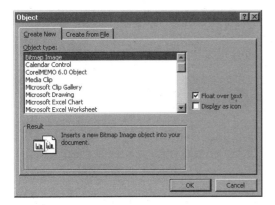

The Object Type list in your dialog box may contain different objects, depending on the programs installed on your computer.

5. Select Microsoft Graph 97 Chart and click OK. Word loads Graph, enters the copied table data in a datasheet, and plots it in a default format, as shown below. (Graph's menu bar and Standard and Formatting toolbars have replaced Word's at the top of the window.)

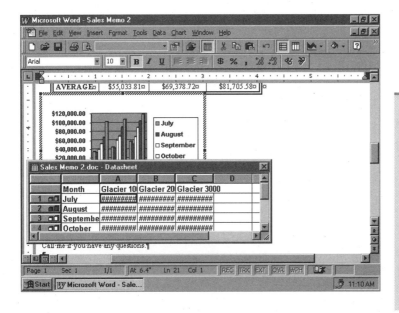

Adding borders to objects

To add a border to any graphic object, select the object, choose the appropriate command from the Format menu or click the corresponding button, and click the Colors And Lines tab. In the Line section, change the Color setting to the desired color, select a style and weight for the border, and then click OK.

6. Click the datasheet's Close button so that you can view all of the graph.

The graph is a little crowded, so let's simplify it by switching from a three-dimensional to a two-dimensional format. (You can work with the graph only when it is selected. If you accidentally click outside the graph, double-click it to reselect it and reactivate the Graph program.) Follow these steps:

The Chart Type button

1. To change the graph type, click the arrow to the right of the Chart Type button on the Graph toolbar to display a palette of options.

2. Click the Column Chart option (the first option in the third row) to change the chart from 3-D to 2-D, as shown here:

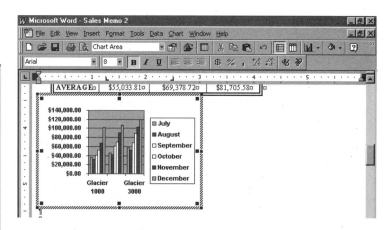

Importing graphs

To import an existing Microsoft Excel graph into a Word document, the graph must be saved in its own file. Choose Object from the Insert menu and click the Create From File tab. Then click the Browse button, navigate to the graph file you want to open, and click OK. Word inserts a copy of the file in your document. To edit the graph, you must double-click it to activate the Graph program. To import a graph created with an application other than Excel, choose Object from the Insert menu, and on the Create New tab, double-click Microsoft Graph 97 Chart to open the Graph program. Clear the contents of the datasheet window (use the Clear command on the Edit menu), click the Import File button on Graph's toolbar, select the file, and click OK.

Not a bad beginning, but the graph obviously needs some adjustments. So that all the labels on the category (x) axis are displayed, let's make the graph object's window a little larger. Try this:

1. Move the pointer over the bottom right corner of the graph, and when it changes to a double-headed arrow, drag the border down and to the right until the graph measures about 4 inches by 2½ inches and all the labels are displayed.

2. Now let's add a title and subtitle. First choose Chart Options from the Chart menu and if necessary, click the Titles tab to display these options:

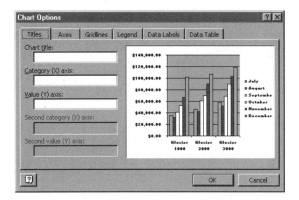

3. Click an insertion point in the Chart Title edit box, type *GLACIER SLEEPING BAGS GROSS SALES*, and click OK.

4. Next select the title text and change the font size to 10 so that the title fits on one line.

5. Click an insertion point at the end of the title, press Enter, and type *July-December 1997*. The graph now looks like this one:

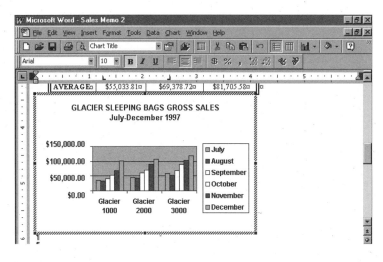

6. Click outside the graph frame to close Microsoft Graph and update the graph in Sales Memo 2.

Returning to your document

When we return to the document in Word, we see that the graph has been inserted below the table but not exactly where we want it. Follow the steps on the next page to make a few more adjustments.

Moving a graph

1. Scroll the window until you see the blank paragraph marks below the graph. Then click the graph once to select it, hold down the left mouse button, and drag down about a ¼ inch. When you release the mouse button, the graph moves down to its new position, and a paragraph mark now separates it from the table.

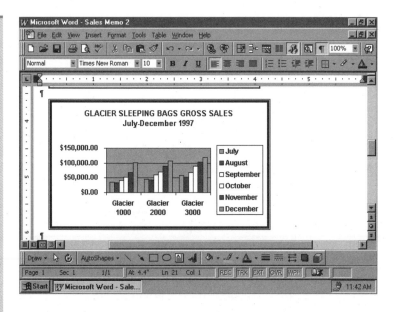

Draw ▾

The Draw button

2. To align the graph with the table above, make sure the graph is still selected and click the Drawing button to display the Drawing toolbar. Then simply click the Draw button and choose Nudge and then Right from the object menu. Repeat this command as necessary. (You can also drag the graph to the right with the mouse or adjust the Horizontal setting on the Position tab of the Format Object dialog box.)

The graph's frame currently has no border. We can add a border by choosing Borders And Shading from the Format menu and then specifying a line color, style, and weight; but here's a simpler way:

Adding a border to a graph

1. With the graph selected, click the Line Style button on the Drawing toolbar and select the first 4½ pt double line option. Here are the results:

More about the Chart Options command

In addition to adding a title to a graph, you can also add or alter many other graph elements using the Chart Options command. On the Axes tab, you can turn off the display of one or both axes. On the Gridlines tab, you can change the display of gridlines. Click the Legend tab to turn off the legend or change its placement. On the Data Labels tab, you can display data labels for each data point in the graph. Finally, on the Data Table tab, you can click the Show Data Table option to display the graph's underlying data as a table below the graph.

2. Click the Save button to safeguard your work.

To edit the graph, we can simply double-click it to open it in Microsoft Graph, where we can change data values in the datasheet, reformat the graph, and change its type.

Editing a graph

Although Graph doesn't offer all the capabilities of dedicated graphing programs, it is often all we need to quickly generate visual representations of our data. You might want to spend a little more time experimenting with this program, using the simple table we created in Chapter 4 or more complex sets of your own data.

Importing Spreadsheets

As we've seen, Word allows us to create impressive tables and perform simple calculations with ease. However, it can't handle complex formulas and functions the way a spreadsheet program can. On the other hand, though a spreadsheet program is great for performing calculations, it lacks the word-processing capabilities needed to put together dynamic reports. Suppose we have gone to a lot of trouble to create a spreadsheet and we want to include the spreadsheet's data in a document. It would be frustrating to have to rekey all that information into a Word table for presentation. Fortunately, we don't have to. With Word 97, we can combine the best of both worlds—the numeric know-how of a spreadsheet program with the word-processing proficiency of Word.

To demonstrate, we'll import the spreadsheet below, which we created with Microsoft Excel 97, into the Sales Memo 2 document.

	3rd Quarter	4th Quarter	Total
1997 GLACIER INCOME			
Sales	$435,622.85	$801,085.75	$1,236,708.60
Selling Expenses	$130,686.86	$240,325.73	$ 371,012.58
Marketing Expenses	$ 43,562.29	$ 80,108.58	$ 123,670.86
Overhead	$ 87,124.57	$160,217.15	$ 247,341.72
Total Expenses	$261,373.71	$480,651.45	$ 742,025.16
Net Income	$174,249.14	$320,434.30	$ 494,683.44

The Insert Microsoft Excel
Worksheet button

To import an Excel file, we can click the Insert Microsoft Excel Worksheet button on the toolbar. But because you might want to import spreadsheets that were created in other programs, we'll show you the most generic method. Follow these steps with your own spreadsheet file (or you can quickly create a version of ours):

1. Click an insertion point to the left of the second blank paragraph mark below the graph in Sales Memo 2. (If necessary, press Enter to add some space.)

2. Choose File from the Insert menu. Word displays the Insert File dialog box.

3. From the Files Of Type drop-down list, select All Files. Move to the folder in which the spreadsheet is stored and double-click the spreadsheet file you want to import. Word displays the dialog box shown here:

Linking data from other applications

You can create a dynamic link between spreadsheet or database information and a Word document either by embedding the information as an object in the Word document or by linking the information to the Word document. To use the embedding technique, choose Object from the Insert menu, and on the Create From File tab, select the file, click Link To File, and click OK. To use the linking technique, open the information in the source application and copy it to the Clipboard. Then switch to the Word document, choose Paste Special from the Edit menu, click Paste Link, specify the type of link, and then click OK. If the linked information changes in its source document, Word will automatically update the Word document when you open it. If the document is already open, you can update the information in the Word document by choosing the Links command from the Edit menu.

4. Either accept the default Entire Workbook option or select a sheet from the Open Document drop-down list. If you select a sheet, you can specify the range you want to import in the Name Or Cell Range edit box. For example, we selected Sheet1 and specified A1:D11 as the range. Click OK to start the conversion process. When Word finishes the conversion, the spreadsheet file is inserted as a table at the insertion point.

5. Format the spreadsheet using the table-formatting techniques described on page 89. Here's how our table looked after we adjusted column widths, added a border, and indented the table:

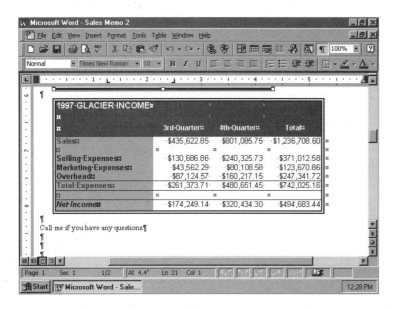

Using only Word's features, you can create some pretty fancy documents. Adding special text effects, a few graphics, and graphs gives those documents real distinction! So be adventurous, and let Word help you generate documents that will make your clients and colleagues sit up and take notice.

Mail Merge:
Form Letters and Labels

It's easy to prepare documents for mail merging with Word. We create a small client database and use it to print some form letters. Next, we create more complex form letters by inserting conditional statements. Finally, we print a set of mailing labels.

1200 Yukon Avenue, Anchorage, AK 99502

Tim Buhr
947 St. Clair Road
Conway, NH 03818

Dear Tim:

Thank you for your recent order of Glacier sleeping bags. Your order of $250 worth of merchandise is greatly appreciated.

We are excited about this new line and
improve upon the standards for our slee
fill out the enclosed questionnaire and r

We appreciate your input and look forw

Sincerely,

Al Pine, President

Print mailing labels using the same set of records

Tim Buhr
947 St. Clair Road
Conway, NH 03818

1200 Yukon Avenue, Anchorage, AK 99502

Brooke Trout
The Great Outdoors Inc.
1432 West Colorado Hwy.
Colorado Springs, CO 80901

Dear Brooke:

Thank you for your recent order of Glacier sleeping bags. Your order of $1,250 worth of merchandise is greatly appreciated. Because of the size of your order, we are offering you an additional 10% off on your next purchase.

We are excited about this new line and are eager to hear your comments. The best way for us to continually improve upon the standards for our sleeping bags is by addressing your comments. Please take a moment to fill out the enclosed questionnaire and return it to us.

We appreciate your input and look forward to doing business with you again.

Sincerely,

Al Pine, President

Create form letters using name and address records in a data source

Print text for records that meet certain conditions

Most people in the United States have received at least a few personalized form letters. Even kids get them! You know the sort of thing—your name is sprinkled liberally throughout, with a few references to the city in which you live or some other item of personal information. Mail of this sort is an example of the use, and often the abuse, of the mail merge feature available with many word-processing programs. We certainly don't want to assist in the destruction of the forests of the world by showing you how to send junk mail to millions of people. But if you'll use your new knowledge wisely and with restraint, we'll introduce you to the mysteries of mail merge.

Actually, with Word 97, mail merge isn't even all that mysterious. If you have used this feature in other word processors or in previous versions of Word, you'll be pleasantly surprised at the ease with which you can now create mail merge documents using Word 97. For those of you who have never used mail merge (or *print merge*, as it is often called), we'll start with a definition.

What Is Mail Merge?

Mail merge is the printing of a bunch of similar documents by merging the information in one document, called the *main document*, with what is essentially a database of variable information in a second document, called the *data source*.

The main document

Merge fields

The main document contains the information that does not change from printout to printout—the text of a form letter, for example—along with placeholders called *merge fields* for the variable information and codes that control the merging process. A main document with a typical set of merge fields is shown at the top of the facing page.

The data source

Each word enclosed in chevrons is a name that matches the name of a field in the corresponding data source, also shown on the facing page. As you can see, the data source contains the information that changes with each printout: first name, last name, company, address, and so on. The data in this particular source document is stored in a Word table, but we can

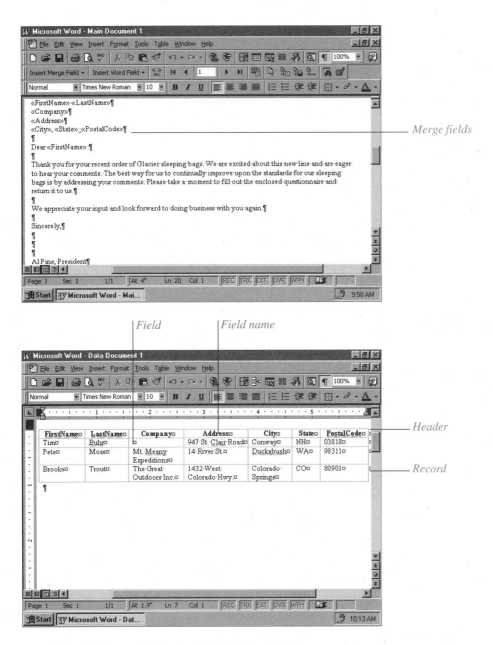

Merge fields

Field Field name

Header

Record

use other formats. (Called *tab-delimited fields* or *comma-delimited fields,* these formats are standard output formats for most spreadsheets and databases.) In the table, each row, which is called a *record*, contains the variable information for one printout. Each cell (the intersection of a column and a

Records

Fields →

Headers and field names →

row), which is called a *field*, contains one variable item, usually a single word or a short phrase. We can include as many records as we want (or as many as disk space permits) in a data source, and the number of fields we can have is practically unlimited. The first record (the top row of the table) is called the *header*. Each field in the header contains a *field name* that identifies the contents of the column below it.

As you'll see later in the chapter, the result of merging the sample main document and data source shown on the previous page is three letters, each with the appropriate information instead of the merge fields. Although mail merge documents can be pretty complex—they can include conditional elements, mathematical calculations, logical comparisons, and branching instructions—most are as simple as the sample documents we'll use in this chapter.

In addition to creating letters, mail merge is a handy tool for filling in forms and is particularly useful when the information needed to fill in the forms is already included in a database or spreadsheet. For example, we might use mail merge to print invoices, checks, and insurance forms, as well as all kinds of labels—for mailings and for collections of disks, audio cassettes, CDs, video tapes, and books. Printing labels of various types is such a common use of mail merge that Word includes instructions to guide us through the process. We'll have a look at labels later. Right now, let's create the sample form letter.

Creating Form Letters

Field location

The order of the fields in the data source is not important to the operation of the mail merge feature. The main document can use any combination of fields in any order. If the order of the data source fields is significant, you can insert them manually where you want them or move them after they have been inserted.

The first stage of creating a form letter is to take a few moments to plan it. We might draft a sample letter and mark all the words or phrases that will vary from letter to letter. Then we might organize our sources of information to make sure we have easy access to all the names, addresses, and other tidbits of information required. Only after these tasks have been completed will we actually create the main document and data source. Assume that we have already taken care of this planning stage for you so that you can now start the interesting part.

Creating the Main Document

Word walks you through the steps for creating four types of main documents: form letters, mailing labels, envelopes, and catalogs. (See page 152 for information about setting up labels, and see the tip on page 148 for a brief discussion of catalogs.) To set up your main document, follow these steps:

1. With Word loaded, choose New from the File menu, click the Letters & Faxes tab, and double-click the icon for the Letter-head template you created in Chapter 5.

2. Click the Save button, and in the Save As dialog box, assign the name *Main Document 1* to the file, and save it in the My Documents folder.

3. Choose Mail Merge from the Tools menu to display the dialog box shown here:

Starting mail merge

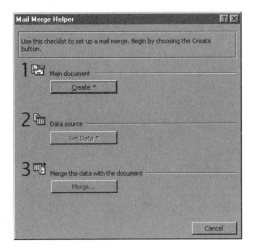

As you can see, Word is ready to lead you through the mail merge process.

4. Follow the suggestion at the top of the dialog box and click the Create button. A list drops down, offering you the choices shown on the next page.

Creating a new main document

You don't have to create the main document before you begin the mail merge operation. After selecting Form Letters from the Create list in the Mail Merge Helper dialog box, simply click New Main Document to open a new document and to add an Edit button to the dialog box. You can then use the Edit button to switch to the main document at any time and type or edit it.

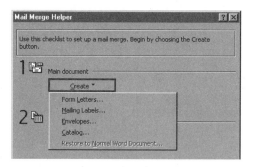

5. Select Form Letters. Word displays this dialog box:

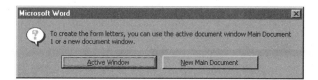

6. Click the Active Window button to use Main Document 1 as your main document.

Now let's create the data source, which will contain all the variable information for the form letters.

Creating the Data Source

With most word processors, we have to create the data source before we begin the mail merge process. With Word, we can either open an existing data source or we can have Word guide us through the procedure for creating one, like this:

1. With the Mail Merge Helper dialog box still open, click the Get Data button to drop down this list of options:

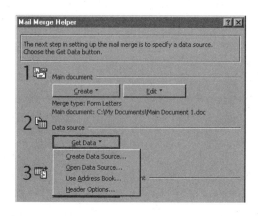

Data source preparation

Before creating the data source for a mail merge document, you should think through how the data source will be used. If you plan on sorting any of your data (see the tip on page 150), you need to put the information you want to sort in separate fields. If you think you may use the data source for different kinds of mail merge documents, you may want to add extra fields that won't be used in one type of document but will in another. For example, in an address label document, you may want to include a job title, such as *Al Pine, President*, but in the salutation of a letter, you may only want to include the first and/or last name (*Dear Al Pine:* or *Dear Al:*). You'll have more flexibility if you include all the information but organize it in separate fields.

2. Select Create Data Source to display this dialog box, which helps set up the fields of the data source:

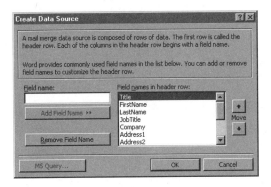

3. The list box on the right displays commonly used field names. You want this data source to have FirstName, LastName, Company, Address, City, State, and PostalCode (Zip) fields. You don't want the selected field name, Title, so click Remove Field Name to delete it from the list. Also remove JobTitle, Address2, Country, HomePhone, and WorkPhone.

Removing field names

4. Now remove Address1 from the list, and then with Address1 in the Field Name edit box, delete the 1 and click Add Field Name to add Address back to the list.

Editing field names

5. With Address still selected, click the Move Up arrow repeatedly to move the Address field up until it is between Company and City. The dialog box now looks like this:

Rearranging field names

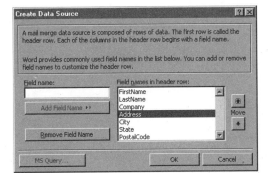

Field name rules

Field names can have as many as 40 characters and can include letters, numbers, and underscore characters. Each field name must start with a letter and cannot contain spaces. To get around the "no spaces" rule, you can assign multiword fields names, such as LastName or Last_Name.

6. Click OK to close the dialog box. Word displays the Save As dialog box so that you can name the new data source.

7. Assign the name *Data Document 1* to the document, and click Save. Word displays this dialog box:

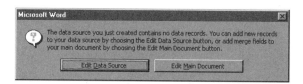

Entering records in
the data source

8. Click the Edit Data Source button to display the Data Form dialog box shown below, where you can begin entering records in the data source:

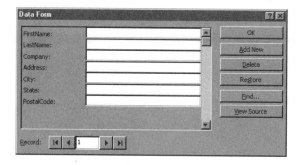

Navigating the Data Form
dialog box

9. Go ahead and enter the information shown in the table on the facing page, pressing either Tab or Enter to move from field to field. After you fill in the last field in one record, click the Add New button or press Enter to move to a new record. You can use the arrows at the bottom of the screen to move back and forth through the records.

Using an existing data source

If you want to use an existing Word document as the data source for your form letters, select Open Data Source from the Get Data list in the Mail Merge Helper dialog box, and then select the file you want to use. (The information in the file must be set up in a table or be separated by tabs or commas for Word to be able to use it as a mail merge data source.) You can also use existing database information from other applications as the data source. Candidates are databases created in certain versions of Microsoft Access, Microsoft Excel, Microsoft FoxPro, and dBASE. The process for opening a database created in another application is basically the same as that for opening a Word document, although a file conversion program (supplied with Word) is often needed to complete the task.

Field	Record1	Record2	Record3
FirstName	Tim	Pete	Brooke
LastName	Buhr	Moss	Trout
Company		Mt. Meany Expeditions	The Great Outdoors Inc.
Address	947 St. Clair Road	14 River St.	1432 West Colorado Hwy.
City	Conway	Duckabush	Colorado Springs
State	NH	WA	CO
PostalCode	03818	98311	80901

10. After entering the three records, click OK. Word closes the dialog box and returns to the main document.

Completing the Main Document

When we return to the main document, the most obvious change is that the Mail Merge toolbar has joined the Standard and Formatting toolbars at the top of the screen. This toolbar makes it easy to add placeholders for the variable information that will be merged from the data source. You might want to move the pointer over its buttons to orient yourself.

The next task is to type the text of the letter, inserting merge field placeholders. Let's start by entering the addressee information, which consists almost entirely of merge fields:

1. Press Ctrl+End to move to the blank paragraph below the letterhead. (If you don't have a blank paragraph, press Enter and then format the new paragraph as left-aligned, 10 point, regular text.)

2. Press Enter to add some space and then click the Insert Merge Field button on the Mail Merge toolbar to drop down a list of the available fields.

3. Click FirstName. The FirstName merge field appears at the insertion point, enclosed in chevrons. (If Word displays {MERGEFIELD FirstName} instead of <<FirstName>>, press Alt+F9 to turn off the display of codes and turn on the display of merge fields. If Word displays the actual first name from your first record, simply click the View Merged Data button on the Mail Merge toolbar to toggle it off and to display the merge field.)

Using electronic address books

When creating a mail merge letter or a set of labels (see page 152), you may want to use addresses entered in an electronic address book, such as the Microsoft Outlook or Microsoft Schedule+ address book. To do so, first select Use Address Book from the Get Data list in the Mail Merge Helper dialog box. Next choose the address book you want to use and click OK. You can then click the Insert Merge Field button in your main document and insert any of the fields available in the address book as merge fields. When creating an envelope or label using the Envelopes And Labels command on the Tools menu (see the tip on page 153), you can access an address book by clicking the Insert Address button above the Address box, selecting the address book you want to use, selecting the desired entry, and clicking OK.

4. Press the Spacebar, click the Insert Merge Field button again, click LastName to insert that merge field, and press Enter to start a new line. Repeat this procedure for the Company merge field and the Address merge field.

5. Click Insert Merge Field, insert City, type a comma and a space, insert State, type two spaces, and insert PostalCode.

6. Press Enter a couple of times, and then type *Dear* and a space.

7. Insert the FirstName merge field, type a colon (:), and press Enter twice. (If necessary, close the Office Assistant.)

8. Now type the body of the letter, as shown here (we turned off the ruler to show more of the screen):

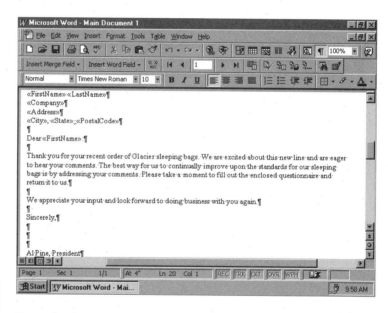

9. Save the document.

Merging the Documents

We are now ready to merge the main document with the data source. We have several options here. Notice the set of four buttons toward the right end of the Mail Merge toolbar. We can click the Check For Errors button so that Word will ascertain whether the main document and data source are set up correctly. If we click the Merge To New Document button,

Formatting merge fields

You can format merge fields the same way you format any text. Simply select the fields and use the buttons on the Formatting toolbar or the character formatting options in the Font dialog box. Then when you merge the main document and the data source, Word applies the formatting specified in the main document to all the merged documents.

Word merges the main document with the data source and puts the resulting letters in a new document that you can save and print later. If we click the Merge To Printer button, Word merges the main document and data source but sends them directly to the printer. If we click the Mail Merge button, Word displays a dialog box in which we can specify where to merge the records, which records to merge, whether blank fields are to be printed, and so on. Let's experiment:

Specifying mail merge options

1. Click the Check For Errors button to display these options:

The Check For Errors button

2. Select the Simulate option and click OK. If you followed our instructions, you'll see a dialog box announcing that Word found no mail merge errors. (Word points out any errors so that you can correct them.) Click OK to return to your document.

3. Now click the Merge To New Document button. Word opens a new document window called *Form Letters1* and then "prints" the letters to the document, with a section break between each letter, like this:

The Merge To New Document button

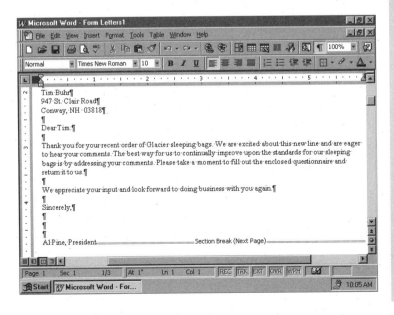

Merging selected records

If your data source contains many records and you want to merge only those records that meet certain criteria (for example, only those with specific Zip codes), you can "filter" the records to extract the ones you want. The filtering process is too complex to discuss thoroughly here, but briefly, you click the Query Options button in the Mail Merge Helper dialog box and specify your criteria on the Filter Records tab. For example, setting PostalCode equal to 98052 filters out for merging all the records in the data source with 98052 in the PostalCode field.

The Merge To Printer button

4. Close Form Letters1, saving it when prompted, with the name *Form Letters*.

5. If your printer is turned on and you want to try the Merge To Printer button, go ahead and click it, and then click OK in the Print dialog box. The printed letters will look like those shown at the beginning of the chapter.

Now that you know how to do simple mail merges, let's look at some more sophisticated mail merge capabilities.

Creating More Sophisticated Letters

We named the main document and data source for this example Main Document 1 and Data Document 1, respectively, but we could have saved them with any valid names. And we can open and edit the documents just like any other documents. The data source is just a normal document that contains a table, so we can add fields and records to this table the same way we can add columns and rows to any table. And we can add tables, charts, pictures, and various types of Word fields to the main document. We can even include fields that cause the mail merge process to pause and prompt for additional information that is not included in the data source.

Word gives us several methods of controlling exactly what is printed in a merged document. Although these methods are not very complicated, a complete explanation of them is beyond the scope of this book. However, we can quickly turn our original form letter into one that makes a decision about what to print, just to give an idea of what can be done.

Adding Fields to the Data Source

Let's create a letter thanking people for their order of Glacier sleeping bags, and include a paragraph that Word will print only if the order is over a certain amount. To allow Word to make the printing decision, we have to add a field to the data source to hold the amount of the order. Follow the steps on the facing page.

Catalogs

When you want to create lists of information using the fields in a data source, select the Catalog option from the main document's Create list in the Mail Merge Helper dialog box. For example, suppose your company wants to create a list of employee names and emergency phone numbers using three fields from a personnel database. After selecting Catalog and identifying the data source, you enter the LastName, FirstName, and EmergencyPhone fields just once in the main document (be sure to press Enter after the last field). When you click the Merge To New Document button on the Mail Merge toolbar, Word creates one document containing the specified information for all the employees in the data source.

1. Because Data Document 1 is just another Word document, open the file as usual to display it in a window on top of the main document.

2. If opening the data source doesn't display the Database toolbar, right-click one of the existing toolbars and choose Database from the object menu. If you don't see gridlines, choose Show Gridlines from the Table menu.

The Manage Fields button

3. Click the Manage Fields button on the Database toolbar to display this dialog box:

4. Type *Order* as the field name, and press Enter. Word adds the field to the bottom of the list and to the right end of the table. Click OK to close the dialog box.

5. Click to the left of the cell marker below Order (not the row marker at the end of the row) and type *$250*. Press the Down Arrow, type *$600*, press the Down Arrow, and type *$1,250*.

The Mail Merge Main
Document button

6. Click the Save button and then click the Mail Merge Main Document button on the Database toolbar to move back to the open main document.

Editing the Main Document

Instead of creating a new main document from scratch, we'll edit the one we've already saved. Here's how:

1. Click an insertion point to the left of the *W* in the second sentence of the letter (the one that begins *We are excited*).

2. Type *Your order of* and press the Spacebar.

3. Click the Insert Merge Field button and select the new Order field. Then type a space followed by *worth of merchandise is greatly appreciated.*

Adding data to the data source

After creating a new field in the data source, you can add the field information in two ways: You can type the information directly in the data source table; or you can click the Data Form button on the Database toolbar to display its dialog box, where you can add the field information to each record in turn.

4. With the insertion point still to the left of the *W* in *We are excited*, press the Spacebar and then press Enter twice, leaving a space after the sentence you just typed.

Next we need to enter the conditional statement that will control printing of an additional sentence based on the amount of the contribution. Follow these steps:

Inserting a conditional statement

1. Click an insertion point after the space at the end of the new sentence, click the Insert Word Field button to drop down a list of fields, and select the If...Then...Else... option. Word displays this dialog box:

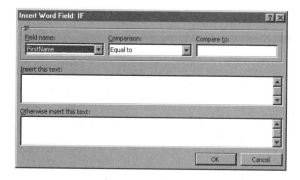

2. Click the arrow to the right of the Field Name edit box to drop down a list of field names. Scroll down to Order and click it to insert it in the Field Name edit box.

3. Drop down the Comparison list and select Greater Than.

4. Click the Compare To edit box and type *500*.

5. Press Tab to move to the Insert This Text box, and type the following:

Because of the size of your order, we are offering you an additional 10% off on your next purchase.

If the result of the conditional statement is true—that is, if the value of the order is greater than $500—Word will enter this text in the merged document.

Sorting data

In some circumstances, you may want to sort the information contained in your data source in a particular order. For example, if you want to print letters in last-name alphabetical order or labels in Zip code order, you can select the appropriate column in the data source document and click the Sort Ascending button on the Database toolbar. For more complex sorts—ones using more than one sort criteria—choose Sort from the Table menu and select the appropriate options.

6. Leave the Otherwise Insert This Text box blank, because you don't want Word to print anything if the conditional statement is not true—that is, if the value of the order is $500 or less.

7. Click OK to close the dialog box, and then press Alt+F9 to turn off the display of merge fields and turn on the display of field codes, which look like this:

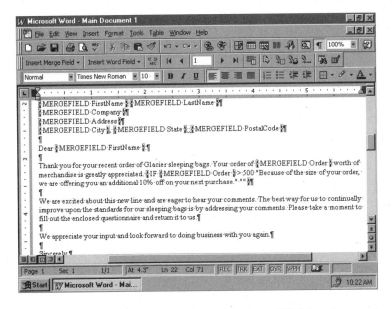

8. Press Alt+F9 again to turn off the display of field codes, and then save the main document as *Main Document 2*.

That's all there is to it. We now have several options to check the results of our efforts. We can click one of the buttons on the Mail Merge toolbar to merge the letters to a document or to the printer, or we can look at the results right in the main document. Try this:

1. Click the View Merged Data button on the Mail Merge toolbar to display the data from the first record in place of the merge fields.

2. Click the right and left arrows on the Mail Merge toolbar to cycle through the records in your data source. (The current

Turning on field codes display

The View Merged Data button

Cycling through records

record number is displayed in the box between the arrows.) The merged data for the third record, which has an order of $1,250, is shown here:

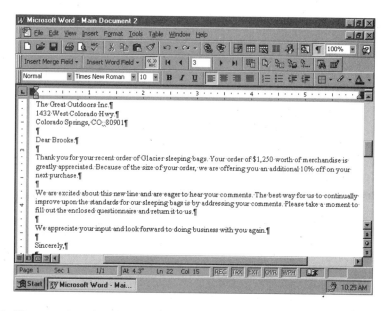

3. If you entered orders of $250, $600, and $1,250 for the three customers, the first customer's letter doesn't have the extra sentence and the second and third letters do. Try changing the comparison operator from > to < (less than) by pressing Alt+F9 to display the field codes, selecting the > symbol, and typing a < in its place. Then press Alt+F9 again and cycle through the records to see the result.

Changing the comparison operator

4. If you want, save the merged document as *Letters*, and then save and close all open documents to prepare for the next example.

Now let's take a look at how the mail merge feature can help us print labels.

Creating Labels

When you used the Mail Merge Helper dialog box to create a form letter, you undoubtedly noticed that it could also be used to create labels and envelopes. In this section, we discuss the procedure for printing multiple labels. (If you want to print just one label or envelope, use the Envelopes And Labels command on the Tools menu, as described in the tip below.) The procedure for printing multiple envelopes is similar to the one we'll describe here; if anything, you'll find that printing envelopes is easier because you have fewer options to deal with.

Follow the steps below to create a set of mailing labels for the sample form letter using the data source we created earlier. (To create other labels, you will first need to set up and save a data source so that you can select it in step 4; see page 142.)

1. Click the New button on the toolbar to create a new document that you can use as the main document for your labels.

2. Choose Mail Merge from the Tools menu to display the Mail Merge Helper dialog box shown earlier on page 141.

3. Click the Create button in the Main Document section and select Mailing Labels from the list of options. When Word asks whether you want to use the active window or create a new document, click Active Window.

4. Back in the Mail Merge Helper dialog box, click the Get Data button in the Data Source section, select Open Data Source from the list of options, and double-click Data Document 1, the source document we created earlier.

5. Word advises that you now need to create the main document. Click Set Up Main Document to display the dialog box shown below, which helps you define the label you want to use:

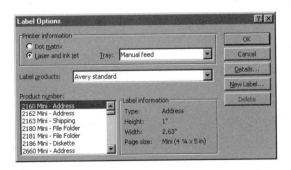

One envelope or label

If you want to print a single envelope or label, choose Envelopes And Labels from the Tools menu. You can then click the tab for either Envelopes or Labels in the resulting dialog box. Click Options to change the envelope or label size and click OK. Then fill in the information you want to appear on the envelope or label and click Print.

Notice that you can select either Dot Matrix or Laser And Ink Jet in the Printer Information section. This setting determines the type of labels displayed in the Product Number list: Laser or ink jet labels typically come on 8-by-11-inch sheets, and dot matrix labels come on fanfold paper.

Displaying information
about a label

6. Scroll through the Product Number list to get an idea of what is available. (You can highlight an item to see general information about it in the adjacent Label Information section. Click the Details button to see more information about the selected label.)

7. Select the 5161 Address label if you have a laser printer or the 4143 Address label if you have a dot matrix printer. Click Details. This dialog box appears for the 5161 Address label:

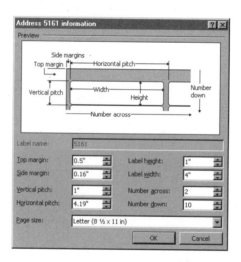

As you can see, the Information dialog box displays a drawing of the selected label, with its characteristics listed below. You can change each characteristic—margins, pitch, height, width, and number across and down—by entering a new value in the corresponding edit box. This flexibility is handy if you want to print labels in a format that isn't included in Word's lists. You can select a format that is similar and then fine-tune it in the Information dialog box.

Other types of labels

In addition to regular address labels, Word can print labels for shipping, file folders, name tags, disks, audio and video tapes, and several types of cards. It is worth exploring whether Word can help automate some of your routine label-making tasks.

8. Go ahead and change the characteristics of this label, and watch the drawing change. (If you click OK, Word asks you

to enter a name for your custom label in the Label Name edit box.) Then click Cancel to close the dialog box without recording your changes.

9. Click OK to close the Label Options dialog box. Word displays this dialog box so that you can create the label format for your main document:

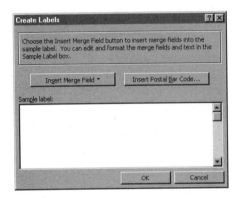

10. Next, create the label format the same way you created the addressee portion of the form letter earlier in the chapter. Click the Insert Merge Field button, select FirstName, press the Spacebar, click Insert Merge Field, select LastName, and press Enter. Then insert the Company, Address, City, State, and PostalCode merge fields, like this:

Inserting merge fields in a label

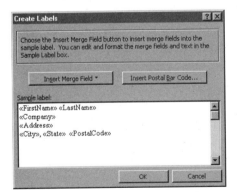

Be sure the bottom line of the label text consists of the three merge fields shown above, with punctuation and spacing included.

Adding bar codes

You can cut down on postage costs for bulk mailings by printing a POSTNET bar code on your labels or envelopes. To insert a bar code, click the Insert Postal Bar Code button in the Create Labels (or Envelope Address) dialog box, select the fields that contain the Zip code and street address (or post office box number), and click OK. Word prints the bar code at the top of the label (or above the address on an envelope).

11. Click OK to return to the Mail Merge Helper dialog box, and then click Merge in the Merge The Data With The Document section to display this dialog box:

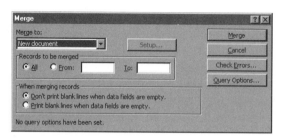

12. Click Merge to merge the labels to a new document rather than the printer. After a couple of seconds, you should see something like this on your screen:

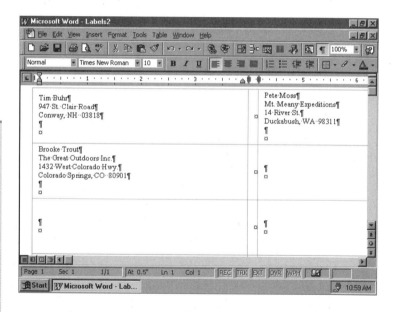

An entire sheet of the same label

Sometimes you may need to print an entire sheet of the same label—for example, for your return address. Choose Envelopes And Labels from the Tools menu. Click the Labels tab and type the desired information on the label in the Address box. Click the Full Page Of The Same Label option in the Print section, click Options to select the label style you are using, and then click OK. Finally, click Print to send the sheet of labels directly to the printer, or click New Document to insert the label information in a document that you can edit, format, and save just like any other Word document.

If you want, save the merged document with a name such as *Label 1* so that you can print it later. Save the main document with a name such as *Label Main Document* so that you can reuse it in the future.

That's all there is to it. You should test-print the labels on plain paper to check their alignment, and then you can replace the paper with label sheets and print away! After you have been through the process once or twice, you will probably find that it takes you less time to merge a batch of labels than it did to read these instructions.

Printing a batch of envelopes is even easier than labels. With a new, blank document displayed on your screen, create a default return address for your envelopes by choosing Envelopes And Labels from the Tools menu, entering a return address in the Return Address box on the Envelopes tab, and clicking Add To Document. When Word asks if you want to save the return address as the default, click Yes. Next, choose Mail Merge from the Tools menu. Select Envelopes from the list that drops down when you click the Create button in the Main Document section of the Mail Merge Helper dialog box, and follow Word's instructions for selecting a data source and setting up the main document in the active window. The first time you create envelopes after specifying the return address, Word warns that it will overwrite the return address displayed in the active document with the mail merge information you just set up. (This does not mean that Word will delete your default return address information.) Click OK and then click the Merge button to merge the envelopes to a new document or to your printer. When you use the Mail Merge command to create envelopes in the future, Word will automatically add the return address to the top left corner of your envelopes.

Printing envelopes

Congratulations! You have now completed your Quick Course in Word. By now you should feel comfortable with most aspects of the program. With the basics you have learned here, together with the Help feature and the sample documents that come with Word, you should be able to tackle the creation of some pretty sophisticated documents. Good luck!

Index

Quick Course®

books—first-class training at
economy prices!

"...perfect to help groups of new users become productive quickly."

—PC Magazine

Perfect for educators and trainers, Quick Course® books offer streamlined instruction for the new user in the form of no-nonsense, to-the-point tutorials and learning exercises. The core of each book is a logical sequence of straightforward, easy-to-follow instructions for building useful business documents—the same documents people create and use on the job.

Microsoft Office 97
U.S.A. **$24.99**
U.K. £22.99
Canada $34.99
ISBN 1-57231-726-4

Microsoft Windows 95
U.S.A. **$14.99**
U.K. £13.99
Canada $20.99
ISBN 1-57231-727-2

Microsoft Word 97
U.S.A. **$14.99**
U.K. £13.99
Canada $20.99
ISBN 1-57231-725-6

Microsoft Excel 97
U.S.A. **$14.99**
U.K. £13.99
Canada $20.99
ISBN 1-57231-723-X

Microsoft Access 97
U.S.A. **$14.99**
U.K. £13.99
Canada $20.99
ISBN 1-57231-722-1

Microsoft PowerPoint 97
U.S.A. **$14.99**
U.K. £13.99
Canada $20.99
ISBN 1-57231-724-8

Microsoft Press® products are available worldwide wherever quality computer books are sold. For more information, contact your book or computer retailer, software reseller, or local Microsoft Sales Office, or visit our Web site at mspress.microsoft.com. To locate your nearest source for Microsoft Press products, or to order directly, call 1-800-MSPRESS in the U.S. (in Canada, call 1-800-268-2222).

Prices and availability dates are subject to change.

Microsoft®*Press*